# Best Practices

SUSE Manager 3.1

Best Practices
SUSE Manager 3.1
Joseph Cayouette

Publication Date: 2017-12-04

Edited by SUSE Manager Team

SUSE LLC
10 Canal Park Drive
Suite 200
Cambridge MA 02141
USA
https://www.suse.com/documentation ↗

Red Hat, Red Hat Enterprise Linux, the Shadowman logo, JBoss, MetaMatrix, Fedora, the Infinity Logo, and RHCE are trademarks of Red Hat, Inc., registered in the United States and other countries. Linux® is the registered trademark of Linus Torvalds in the United States and other countries. Java® is a registered trademark of Oracle and/or its affiliates. XFS® is a trademark of Silicon Graphics International Corp. or its subsidiaries in the United States and/or other countries. MySQL® is a registered trademark of MySQL AB in the United States, the European Union and other countries. All other trademarks are the property of their respective owners.

For SUSE trademarks, see http://www.suse.com/company/legal/ ↗. All other third-party trademarks are the property of their respective owners. Trademark symbols (®, ™ etc.) denote trademarks of SUSE and its affiliates. Asterisks (*) denote third-party trademarks.

All information found in this book has been compiled with utmost attention to detail. However, this does not guarantee complete accuracy. Neither SUSE LLC, its affiliates, the authors nor the translators shall be held liable for possible errors or the consequences thereof.

# Contents

# 1 Introduction

This document targets system administrators.

## 1.1 What's Covered in this Guide?

This document describes SUSE recommended best practices for SUSE Manager. This information has been collected from a large number of successful SUSE Manager real world implementations and includes feedback provided by product management, sales and engineering.

This chapter will discuss the following topics:

- Prerequisites

- Network Requirements

- Hardware Requirements

## 1.2 Prerequisites

**Purchased Registration Keys.**  During initial setup SUSE Manager will request a product `Registration Key`. This key will be provided to you after purchasing the product. You can find your key located under your SUSE Customer Center account. Log-in with your SUSE Customer Center credentials or register for a new account. — https://scc.suse.com ↗

**Evaluation Keys.**  If you wish to run a test system (non-production) a 60 day evaluation key may be obtained. On the SUSE Manager product page click *TRY SUSE MANAGER*. The evaluation key limits the number of systems that may be registered with SUSE Manager to 10. — https:// www.suse.com/products/suse-manager/ ↗

**SCC Organization Credentials.**  During setup you will also be asked to enter your SUSE Customer Center `Organization Credentials`.

**Users and Passwords.**  During both the SUSE Linux Enterprise installation and setup of SUSE Manager several users and passwords will be created:

- SUSE Linux Enterprise root user account

- PostgreSQL database user and password

- Certificate of Authority password

- SUSE Manager administrator user and password

 Tip: Safe Passwords

Maintain security by creating safe passwords. Store passwords within a secure location. Use the following guidelines when creating your passwords.

- At least 8 characters long

- Should contain uppercase characters **A B C**

- Should contain lowercase characters **a b c**

- Should contain numbers **1 2 3**

- Should contain symbols **~ ! @ #**

## 1.3 Network Requirements

SUSE Manager and SUSE Manager Proxy both contact several external addresses in order to maintain updates and subscriptions. The following lists provide the up-to-date hostnames for each service requiring permission when used in combination with corporate firewall and content filters.

SUSE CUSTOMER CENTER HOSTNAMES (REQUIRED)

- https://scc.suse.com ↗

- https://updates.suse.com ↗

NOVELL CUSTOMER CENTER HOSTNAMES (LEGACY)

- https://secure-www.novell.com ↗

- https://nu.novell.com ↗

For SUSE Manager to function properly it requires the following pre-configured components within your network.

**Important: Websocket Support**

If SUSE Manager is accessed via an HTTP proxy (Squid, etc) the proxy must support websocket connections.

**Networking Hardware.** The following table provides networking hardware info. As SUSE Manager will likely be managing a large number of systems (quite possibly numbering in hundreds or even thousands), networking hardware which increases bandwidth will become increasingly more important.

| Hardware | Recommended |
|---|---|
| 100Mbits/s Link | Non-production test server |
| 1Gb/s Link + | Production Server |

**DHCP Server.** The purpose of the Dynamic Host Configuration Protocol (DHCP) is to assign network settings centrally (from a server) rather than configuring them locally on each and every workstation. A host configured to use DHCP does not have control over its own static address. It is enabled to configure itself completely and automatically according to directions from the server. A DHCP server supplies not only the IP address and the netmask, but also the host name, domain name, gateway, and name server addresses for the client to use. For more information on configuring DHCP see also:

- https://www.suse.com/documentation/sles-12/book_sle_admin/data/cha_dhcp.html ↗

**FQDN.** DNS assists in assigning an IP address to one or more names and assigning a name to an IP address. In Linux, this conversion is usually carried out by a special type of software known as bind. The machine that takes care of this conversion is called a *name server*. The names make up a hierarchical system in which each name component is separated by a period. The name hierarchy is, however, independent of the IP address hierarchy described above. Consider a complete name, such as jupiter.example.com, written in the format hostname.domain. A full name, referred to as a *fully qualified domain name* (FQDN), consists of a host name and a domain name (example.com). For more information on configuring a name server see also:

- https://www.suse.com/documentation/sles-12/
  book_sle_admin/data/sec_basicnet_nameres.html ↗

**DNS Server.** DNS (domain name system) is required for resolving domain names and host names into IP addresses. For example, the IP address 192.168.2.100 could be assigned to the host name jupiter. In the case of SUSE Manager the DNS server must be resolvable both via DNS and reverse lookup. For more information on configuring DNS see also:

- https://www.suse.com/documentation/sles-12/book_sle_admin/data/cha_dns.html ↗

 Important: Microsoft NT Lan Manager Compatibility

Microsoft NT Lan Manager can be configured for use with basic authentication and will work with SUSE Manager but authentication using native (NTLM) Microsoft protocols is not supported.

**Open Port List.** During the setup process of SUSE Manager all required ports will be opened automatically. The following tables provide you with an overview of ports which are used by SUSE Manager.

TABLE 1.1: REQUIRED SERVER PORTS

| Port | Description |
|------|-------------|
| 67 | Required when SUSE Manager is configured as a DHCP server for systems requesting IP addresses. |
| 69 | Used when SUSE Manager is configured as a PXE server and allows installation and re-installation of PXE-boot enabled systems. |
| 80 | Used to contact SUSE Customer Center. All WebGUI, client, and proxy server requests travel via http or https. |
| 443 | All WebGUI, client, and proxy server requests via http or https and SUSE Manager uses this port for SUSE Customer Center inbound traffic. |
| 5222 | When you wish to push actions to clients this port is required by the osad daemon running on your client systems |
| 5269 | Needed if you push actions to or via a SUSE Manager Proxy. |

| Port | Description |
|------|-------------|
| 4505 | Required by the Salt-master to accept communication requests via TCP from minions. Inbound. |
| 4506 | Required by the Salt-master to accept communication requests via TCP from minions. Inbound. |

For more information, see *Book "Advanced Topics", , Section A.1 "SUSE Manager Server"*.

 Tip: Denying External Network Access

When your network requires denying external network access to and from SUSE Manager, an SMT Server may be registered against SUSE Manager. The SMT server can then be used to synchronize the necessary SUSE repositories. For more information on utilizing an SMT Server, see: *Section 2.2, "Subscription Management Tool (SMT) and Disconnected Setup (DMZ)"*.

 Note: Blocking Port 80

Port 80 may be blocked as traffic is automatically redirected through port 443. It should be noted you will lose redirection. Keep in mind you will need additional ports open when using traditional clients in combination with osad (XMPP TCP 5222).

## 1.4  Hardware Recommendations

This section provides tested production recommendations for small to mid size networks that will be managed by SUSE Manager.

| Hardware | Recommended |
|----------|-------------|
| CPU | Multi-core 64bit CPU (x86_64, ppc64le). |
| RAM | Minimum 4 GB+ for test server<br>Minimum 16 GB+ for base installation<br>Minimum 32 GB+ for a production server |

| Hardware | Recommended |
| --- | --- |
| Free Disk Space | Minimum 100 GB for root partition |
| | Minimum 50 GB for `/var/lib/pgsql` |
| | Minimum 50 GB per SUSE product + 200 GB per Red Hat product `/var/spacewalk` |

**Advised Number of CPUs.** Review the following list for CPU recommendations.

- Connecting 200 systems or less to SUSE Manager: 4 CPUs

- Connecting 500 systems or less to SUSE Manager: 4-8 CPUs

- When implementing RHEL channels: 8 CPUs

**Disk Space.** SUSE Manager stores information in several directories. For these directories it is strongly recommend that you create separate file-systems or use an NFS share. During installation one VG will be created that contains all disks selected during installation. Therefore the first disk should be large enough to contain the OS. Normally 20GB - 50GB is sufficient. A 50 GB partition would be the recommended size. The following directories should be created on a separate file-system.

- `/var/spacewalk` This directory will contain all rpm's. Each RPM will be stored only once. The needed size will depend on the number of channels and type of channels that will be downloaded. The general rule would be that per SUSE Service Pack (including SUSE Red-Hat Expanded Support) around 50 GB should be enough. An extra 150 GB for RES/CentOS repositories should be added on top. If other non-enterprise distributions (eg OpenSUSE) are added, calculated 50 GB per distribution. This directory could also be stored on an NFS share.

- `/var/lib/pgsql` This directory contains the PostgreSQL database. Recommended is to create a file-system of 50 GB. This volume should be monitored, because a full file-system where the database is running on can cause unexpected errors (and this even months after it happened).

- `/srv/tftpboot` If PXE/cobbler is used, this directory will contain the images (initrd and linux) for all created auto-installation profiles. Each image is around 50 MB. Depending on the number of profiles a decision has to be made if it would be useful to move this directory to a separate file-system.

- `/var/log` As SUSE Manager writes a large number of logs, it is recommended to create a separate file-system for /var/log. The size should be around 20 GB.

- `/var/spacewalk/db_backup` For the backup of the PostgreSQL database, it is recommended the create a separate directory. As the database can be rather large, it is advised to mount it on a separate file-system. A safe estimate would be to provide twice space as for the directory created for `/var/lib/pqsql`.

**Supported Databases.** SUSE Manager 3 no longer provides support for an external Oracle database. The default database is an embedded PostgreSQL. During SUSE Manager setup the database will be created and configured.

# 2 Managing Your Subscriptions

There are two methods for managing your subscriptions. Both methods access SUSE Customer Center and provide specialized benefits.

- Directly connecting to SUSE Customer Center is the recommended default way of managing your SUSE Manager Server.

- If you have special network security requirements which do not allow access from your internal network to the internet then you may use a SUSE Linux Enterprise 12 Server running the Subscription Management Tool (SMT). This tool will contact SUSE Customer Center from a system connected to the external network and obtain updates for your clients which you may then mount on your internal SUSE Manager Server. This is the preferred method for managing client systems within a highly secure network infrastructure.

## 2.1 SUSE Customer Center (SCC)

SUSE Customer Center (SCC) is the central place to manage your purchased SUSE subscriptions, helping you access your update channels and get in contact with SUSE experts. The user-friendly interface gives you a centralized view of all your SUSE subscriptions, allowing you to easily find all subscription information you need. The improved registration provides faster access to your patches and updates. SUSE Customer Center is also designed to provide a common platform for your support requests and feedback. Discover a new way of managing your SUSE account and subscriptions via one interface—anytime, anywhere. For more information on using SUSE Customer Center see: https://scc.suse.com/docs/userguide ↗

## 2.2 Subscription Management Tool (SMT) and Disconnected Setup (DMZ)

If it is not possible to connect SUSE Manager directly or via a proxy to the Internet, a disconnected setup in combination with Subscription Management Tool (SMT) is the recommended solution. In this scenario, SMT stays in an "external" network with a connection to SUSE Customer Center and synchronizes the software channels and repositories on a removable storage medium. Then you separate the storage medium from SMT, and mount it locally on your SUSE Manager server to read the updated data.

The following procedure will guide you through using SMT.

PROCEDURE 2.1: SMT: FETCHING REPOSITORY DATA FROM SUSE CUSTOMER CENTER

1. Configure SMT in the external network with SUSE Customer Center (SCC). For details about configuring SMT with SUSE Linux Enterprise 12, see: https://www.suse.com/documentation/sles-12/book_smt/data/book_smt.html ↗

2. Using SMT, mirror all required repositories.

3. Create a "database replacement file" (for example, `/tmp/dbrepl.xml`.

   ```
   smt-sync --createdbreplacementfile /tmp/dbrepl.xml
   ```

4. Mount a removable storage medium such as an external hard disk or USB flash drive.

5. Export the data to the mounted medium:

   ```
   smt-sync --todir /media/disk/
   smt-mirror --dbreplfile /tmp/dbrepl.xml --directory /media/disk \
           --fromlocalsmt -L /var/log/smt/smt-mirror-export.log
   ```

    Important: Write Permissions for SMT User

   The directory being written too must be writeable for the same user as the smt daemon (user=smt). The smt user setting is defined in `/etc/smt.conf`. You can check if the correct user is specified via the following command:

   ```
   # egrep '^smtUser' /etc/smt.conf
   ```

    Note: Keeping A Disconnected Server Up-to-date

   **smt-sync** also exports your subscription data. To keep SUSE Manager up-to-date with your subscriptions, you must frequently import and export this data.

6. Unmount the storage medium and carry it securely to your SUSE Manager 3.1 Server.

The next procedure will show you how to update your server from the SMT media.

PROCEDURE 2.2: UPDATING YOUR SUSE MANAGER SERVER FROM THE STORAGE MEDIUM

1. Mount the storage medium on your SUSE Manager server (for example, at `/media/disk`).

2. Specify the local path on the SUSE Manager server in `/etc/rhn/rhn.conf`:

```
server.susemanager.fromdir = /media/disk
```

This setting is mandatory for SUSE Customer Center and **mgr-sync**.

3. Restart Tomcat:

```
systemctl restart tomcat
```

4. Before performing another operation on the server execute a full sync:

```
mgr-sync refresh    # SCC (fromdir in rhn.conf required!)
```

5. **mgr-sync** can now be executed normally:

```
mgr-sync list channels
mgr-sync add channel channel-label
```

 Warning: Data Corruption

The disk must always be available at the same mount point. To avoid data corruption, do not trigger a sync, if the storage medium is not mounted. If you have already added a channel from a local repository path, you will not be able to change its URL to point to a different path afterwards.

Up-to-date data is now available on your SUSE Manager server and is ready for updating client systems. According to your maintenance windows or update schedule refresh the data on the storage medium with SMT.

**PROCEDURE 2.3: REFRESHING DATA ON THE STORAGE MEDIUM FROM SMT**

1. On your SUSE Manager server, unmount the storage medium and carry it to your SMT.

2. On your SMT system, continue with *Step 4*.

 Warning: Data Corruption

The storage medium must always be available at the same mount point. To avoid data corruption, do not trigger a sync if the storage medium is not mounted.

This concludes using SMT with SUSE Manager 3.1.

# 3 Expanded Support

In the following sections find information about Red Hat and Centos clients.

## 3.1 Managing RES Clients

The following sections provide guidance on managing Red Hat Expanded Support clients, this includes Salt minions and traditional systems.

### 3.1.1 Server Configuration for RES Channels

This section provides guidance on server configuration for RES Channels provided by SUSE.

- Minimum of 8 GB RAM and at least two physical or virtual CPUs. Taskomatic will use one of these CPUs.

- Taskomatic requires of minimum of 3072 MB RAM. This should be set in /etc/rhn/ rhn.conf:

```
taskomatic.java.maxmemory=3072
```

- Provision enough disk space. /var/spacewalk contains all mirrored RPMs. For example, RES 6 x86_64 channels require 90 GB and more.

- LVM or an NFS mount is recommended.

- Access to RHEL 5/6/7 Subscription Media.

### Warning: Access to RHEL Media or Repositories

Access to Red Hat base media repositories and RHEL installation media is the responsibility of the user. Ensure that all your RHEL systems obtain support from RHEL or all your RHEL systems obtain support from SUSE. If you do not follow these practices you may violate terms with Red Hat.

### 3.1.2 RES Channel Management Tips

This section provides tips on RES channel management.

- The base parent distribution RES channel per architecture contains zero packages. No base media is provided by SUSE. The RHEL media or installation ISOs should be added as child channels of the RES parent channel.

- The RES and tools channels are provided by SUSE Customer Center (SCC) using `mgr-sync`.

- It can take up to 24 hours for an initial channel synchronization to complete.

- When you have completed the initial synchronization process of any RES channel it is recommended to clone the channel before working with it. This provides you with a backup of the original synchronization.

## 3.1.3 Mirroring RHEL Media into a Channel

The following procedure guides you through setup of the RHEL media as a SUSE Manager channel. All packages on the RHEL media will be mirrored into a child channel located under RES 5/6/7 distribution per architecture.

PROCEDURE 3.1: MIRRORING RHEL MEDIA INTO A CHANNEL

1. Create a new Channel by log in to the Web UI and selecting *Channels > Manage Software Channels > Create Channel.*

2. Fill in basic channel details and add the channel as a child to the corresponding RES 5/6/7 distribution channel per architecture from SCC. The base parent channel should contain zero packages.

3. Modify the RES 5/6/7 activation key to include this new child channel.

4. As `root` on the SUSE Manager command line copy the ISO to the `/tmp` directory.

5. Create a directory to contain the media content:

```
root # mkdir -p /srv/www/htdocs/pub/rhel
```

6. Mount the ISO:

```
root # mount -o loop /tmp/name_of_iso /srv/www/htdocs/pub/rhel
```

7. Start **spacewalk-repo-sync** to synchronize packages:

```
root # spacewalk-repo-sync -c channel_name -u https://127.0.0.1/pub/rhel/Server/
```

```
Repo URL: https://127.0.0.1/pub/rhel/Server/
Packages in repo:              3690
Packages already synced:          0
Packages to sync:              3690
1/3690 : texlive-latex-2007-57.el6_2-0.x86_64
2/3690 : boost-filesystem-1.41.0-18.el6-0.i686
3/3690 : policycoreutils-newrole-2.0.83-19.39.el6-0.x86_64
[...]
```

8. When the channel has completed the synchronization process you can use the channel as any normal SUSE Manager channel.

## 3.1.4 Registering RES Salt Minions with SUSE Manager

This section will guide you through registering RHEL minions with SUSE Manager. This section assumes you have updated your server to the latest patch level.

### 3.1.4.1 Synchronizing Appropriate RES Channels

Ensure you have the corresponding RES product enabled and required channels have been fully synchronized:

RHEL 7.X

- Product: RES 7

- Mandatory channels: `rhel-x86_64-server-7`, `res7-suse-manager-tools-x86_64`, `res7-x86_64` systemitem >

RHEL 6.X

- Product: RES 6

- Mandatory channels: `rhel-x86_64-server-6`, `res6-suse-manager-tools-x86_64`, `res6-x86_64`

Tip: Checking Synchronization Progress

To check if a channel has finished synchronizing you can do one of the following:

- From the SUSE Manager Web UI browse to *Admin* › *Setup Wizard* and select the *SUSE Products* tab. Here you will find a percent completion bar for each product.

- Alternatively, you may check the synchronization log file located under `/var/log/rhn/reposync/`*`channel-label`*`.log` using cat or the tailf command. Keep in mind that base channels can contain multiple child channels. Each of these child channels will generate its own log during the synchronization progress. Do not assume a channel has finished synchronizing until you have checked all relevant log files including base and child channels.

Create an activation key associated with the RES channel.

### 3.1.4.2 Creating a Bootstrap Repository

The following procedure demonstrate creating a bootstrap repository for RHEL

1. On the server command line as root, create a bootstrap repo for RHEL with the following command:

   ```
   mgr-create-bootstrap-repo RHEL_activation_channel_key
   ```

2. Rename **bootstrap.sh** to **resversion-boostrap.sh**:

   ```
   root # cp bootstrap.sh res7-bootstrap.sh
   ```

### 3.1.5 Register a Salt Minion via Bootstrap

The following procedure will guide you through registering a Salt minion using the bootstrap script.

PROCEDURE 3.2: REGISTRATION USING THE BOOTSTRAP SCRIPT

1. For your new minion download the bootstrap script from the SUSE Manager server:

   ```
   wget --no-check-certificate https://server/pub/bootstrap/res7-bootstrap.sh
   ```

2. Add the appropriate res-gpg-pubkey-#####-#####.key to the `ORG_GPG_KEY` key parameter, comma delimited in your **res7-bootstrap.sh** script. These are located on your SUSE Manager server at:

```
http://server/pub/
```

3. Make the **res7-bootstrap.sh** script executable and run it. This will install necessary Salt packages from the bootstrap repository and start the Salt minion service:

```
root # chmod +x res7-bootstrap.sh
root # ./res7-boostrap.sh
```

4. From the SUSE Manager Web UI select *Salt › Keys* and accept the new minion's key.

> ❗ **Important: Troubleshooting Bootstrap**
>
> If bootstrapping a minion fails it is usually caused by missing packages. These missing packages are contained on the RHEL installation media. The RHEL installation media should be loop mounted and added as a child channel to the RES channel. See the warning in *Section 3.1, "Managing RES Clients"* on access to RHEL Media.

## 3.1.6 Manual Salt Minion Registration

The following procedure will guide you through the registration of a Salt minion manually.

1. Add the bootstrap repository:

```
yum-config-manager --add-repo https://server/pub/repositories/res/7/bootstrap
```

2. Install the `salt-minion` package:

```
root # yum install salt-minion
```

3. Edit the Salt minion configuration file to point to the SUSE Manager server:

```
root # mkdir /etc/salt/minion.d
root # echo "master: server_fqdn" > /etc/salt/minion.d/susemanager.conf
```

4. Start the minion service:

```
root # systemctl start salt-minion
```

5. From the SUSE Manager Web UI select the *Salt › Keys* and accept the new minion's key.

## 3.2 Preparing Channels and Repositories for CentOS Traditional Clients

This following section provides an example procedure for configuring CentOS channels and repositories and finally registering a CentOS client with SUSE Manager. These steps will be identical for Scientific Linux and Fedora.

**PROCEDURE 3.3: PREPARING CHANNELS AND REPOSITORIES**

1. As `root` install `spacewalk-utils` on your SUSE Manager server:

```
zypper in spacewalk-utils
```

 Important: Supported Tools

The `spacewalk-utils` package contains a collection of upstream command line tools which provide assistance with spacewalk administrative operations. You will be using the **spacewalk-common-channels** tool. Keep in mind SUSE only provides support for **spacewalk-clone-by-date** and **spacewalk-manage-channel-life-cycle** tools.

2. Run the **spacewalk-common-channels** script to add the CentOS7 base, updates, and Spacewalk client channels.

```
root # spacewalk-common-channels -u admin -p secret -a x86_64 'centos7'
root # spacewalk-common-channels -u admin -p secret -a x86_64 'centos7-updates'
root # spacewalk-common-channels -u admin -p secret -a x86_64 'spacewalk26-client-centos7'
```

 Note: Required Channel References

The `/etc/rhn/spacewalk-common-channels.ini` must contain the channel references to be added. If a channel is not listed, check the latest version here for updates: https://github.com/spacewalkproject/spacewalk/tree/master/utils ↗

3. From the Web UI select *Software > Manage Software Channels > Overview*. Select the base channel you want to synchronize, in this case `CentOS7 (x86_64)`. Select *Repositories > Sync*. Check the channels you want to synchronize and then click the *Sync Now* button or, optionally, schedule a regular synchronization time.

4. Copy all relevant GPG keys to `/srv/www/htdocs/pub`. Depending on what distribution you are interested in managing these could include an EPEL key, SUSE keys, Red Hat keys, and CentOS keys. After copying these you can reference them in a comma-delimited list within your bootstrap script (see *Procedure 3.4, "Preparing the Bootstrap Script"*).

   - **CentOS7 key files:** http://mirror.centos.org/centos/RPM-GPG-KEY-CentOS-7 ↗

   - **EPEL key file:** http://mirrors.kernel.org/fedora-epel/RPM-GPG-KEY-EPEL-7 ↗

   - **Spacewalk key:** http://spacewalk.redhat.com/yum/RPM-GPG-KEY-spacewalk-2015 ↗

   - **Red Hat keys:** http://www.redhat.com/contact/security-response-team/gpg-keys.html ↗

5. Install and setup a CentOS 7 client with the default installation packages.

6. Ensure the client machine can resolve itself and your SUSE Manager server via DNS. Validate that there is an entry in `/etc/hosts` for the real IP address of the client.

7. Create an activation key (`centos7`) on the SUSE Manager server that points to the correct parent/child channels, including the CentOS base repo, updates, and Spacewalk client.

Now prepare the bootstrap script.

**PROCEDURE 3.4: PREPARING THE BOOTSTRAP SCRIPT**

1. Create/edit your bootstrap script to correctly reflect the following:

```
# can be edited, but probably correct (unless created during initial install):

# NOTE: ACTIVATION_KEYS *must* be used to bootstrap a client machine.

ACTIVATION_KEYS=1-centos7

ORG_GPG_KEY=res.key,RPM-GPG-KEY-CentOS-7,suse-307E3D54.key,suse-9C800ACA.key,RPM-GPG-KEY-spacewalk-2015

FULLY_UPDATE_THIS_BOX=0

yum clean all
```

```
# Install the prerequisites
yum -y install yum-rhn-plugin rhn-setup
```

2. Add the following lines to the bottom of your script, (just before `echo "-bootstrap complete -"` ):

```
# This section is for commands to be executed after registration
mv /etc/yum.repos.d/Cent* /root/
yum clean all
chkconfig rhnsd on
chkconfig osad on
service rhnsd restart
service osad restart
```

3. Continue by following normal bootstrap procedures to bootstrap the new client.

# 3.3   Registering CentOS Salt Minions with SUSE Manager

The following procedure will guide you through registering a CentOS Minion.

 ## Warning: Support for CentOS Patches

CentOS uses patches originating from CentOS is not officially supported by SUSE. See the matrix of SUSE Manager clients on the main page of the SUSE Manager wiki, linked from the *Quick Links* section: https://wiki.microfocus.com/index.php?title=SUSE_Manager ⌐

**PROCEDURE 3.5: REGISTER A CENTOS 7 MINION**

1. Add the Open Build Service repo for Salt:

```
root # yum-config-manager --add-repo http://download.opensuse.org/repositories/
systemsmanagement:/saltstack:/products/RHEL_7/
```

2. Import the repo key:

```
root # rpm --import http://download.opensuse.org/repositories/systemsmanagement:/
saltstack:/products/RHEL_7/repodata/repomd.xml.key
```

3. Check if there is a different repository that contains Salt. If there is more than one repository listed disable the repository that contains Salt apart from the OBS one.

```
root # yum list --showduplicates salt
```

4. Install the Salt minion:

```
root # yum install salt salt-minion
```

5. Change the Salt configuration to point to the SUSE Manager server:

```
root # mkdir -p /etc/salt/minion.d
root # echo "master: server_fqdn" > /etc/salt/minion.d/susemanager.conf
```

6. Restart the minion

```
root # systemctl restart salt-minion
```

7. Proceed to *Salt › Keys* from the Web UI and accept the minion's key.

# 4 Salt Formulas and SUSE Manager

This chapter provides an introduction for using Salt Formulas with SUSE Manager. Creation of custom formulas will also be introduced.

## 4.1 What are Salt Formulas?

Formulas are collections of Salt States that have been pre-written by other Salt users and contain generic parameter fields. Formulas allow for reliable reproduction of a specific configuration again and again. Formulas can be installed from RPM binaries or an external git repository.

The following list should help you in making the decision to use a state or a formula.

FORMULA TIPS

- When writing states for trivial tasks, formulas are probably not worth the time investment.

- For large, non-trivial configurations use formulas.

- Formulas and States both act as a kind of configuration documentation. Once written and stored you will have a snapshot of what your infrastructure should look like.

- You can greatly decrease the amount of time required for writing a formula by grabbing one of the many pre-written formulas on github. There are pre-written formulas for hundreds of configurations. You can find these located at https://github.com/saltstack-formulas ↗.

> **!** **Important: Creating Formulas as a Time Investment**
>
> Creating formulas is possibly one of the most time consuming tasks for a SUSE Manager administrator. However utilizing well designed formulas provides excellent pay-offs, as managing thousands of systems becomes a maintainable, and more importantly a reproducible task. You can find many community prepared formulas and examples at the official Saltstack repository located on github: https://github.com/saltstack-formulas ↗

## 4.2 Installing Salt Formulas via RPM

SUSE releases formulas as RPM packages. These may be installed using zypper.

Note: Formula Channel Location

Available formulas can be located within the `SUSE-Manager-Server-3.1-Pool` channel.

PROCEDURE 4.1: INSTALLING SALT FORMULAS FROM AN RPM

1. To search for available formulas, execute the following command on your SUSE Manager server:

```
# zypper se formula
```

You will be presented with a list of available Salt Formulas:

```
S | Name            | Summary                                                   |
  Type
--+-----------------+-----------------------------------------------------------
+-----------
  | locale-formula  | Locale Salt Formula for SUSE Manager                      |
package
  | locale-formula  | Locale Salt Formula for SUSE Manager                      |
srcpackage
```

2. For more information (metadata) about a specific formula run from the command line as root or with sudo:

```
# zypper info locale-formula
```

```
Information for package locale-formula:
----------------------------------------
Repository: SUSE-Manager-Server-3.1-Pool
Name:  locale-formula
Version:  0.2-1.1
Arch: noarch
Vendor:  SUSE LLC <https://www.suse.com/>
Support Level: Level 3
Status: not installed
Installed Size: 47.9 KiB
Installed: No
Source package : locale-formula-0.2-1.1.src
Summary        : Locale Salt Formula for SUSE Manager
Description    : Salt Formula for SUSE Manager. Sets up the locale.
```

3. To install a formula, as root or with sudo run:

```
# zypper in locale-formula
```

## 4.3  File Structure Overview

RPM-based formulas need to be placed within a specific directory structure to ensure proper functionality. A formula always consists of two separate directories: The `states` directory and the `metadata` directory. Folders in these directories need to have an exactly matching name, for example `locale`.

**The Formula State Directory**

The formula states directory contains anything necessary for a Salt state to work independently. This includes `.sls` files, a `map.jinja` file and any other required files. This directory should only be modified by RPMs and should not be edited manually. For example, the `locale-formula` states directory is located in:

```
/usr/share/susemanager/formulas/states/locale/
```

**The Formula Metadata Directory**

The metadata directory contains a `form.yml` file which defines the forms for SUSE Manager and an optional `metadata.yml` file that can contain additional information about a formula. For example, the `locale-formula` metadata directory is located in:

```
/usr/share/susemanager/formulas/metadata/locale/
```

**Custom Formulas**

Custom formula data or (non-RPM) formulas need to be placed into any state directory configured as a Salt file root:

**State directory**

Custom state formula data need to be placed in:

```
/srv/salt/custom/
```

**Metadata Directory**

Custom metadata (information) need to be placed in:

```
/srv/salt/formula_metadata/custom/
```

All custom folders located in the following directories needs to contain a `form.yml` file. These files are detected as form recipes and may be applied to groups and systems from the Web UI:

```
/srv/formula_data/custom-formula-name/form.yml
```

## 4.4 Editing Pillar Data in SUSE Manager

SUSE Manager requires a file called `form.yml`, to describe how formula data should look within the Web UI. `form.yml` is used by SUSE Manager to generate the desired form, with values editable by a user.

For example, the `form.yml` that is included with the `locale-formula` is placed in:

```
/usr/share/susemanager/formulas/metadata/locale/form.yml
```

See part of the following `locale-formula` example:

```
# This file is part of locale-formula.
#
# Foobar is free software: you can redistribute it and/or modify
# it under the terms of the GNU General Public License as published by
# the Free Software Foundation, either version 3 of the License, or
# (at your option) any later version.
#
# Foobar is distributed in the hope that it will be useful,
# but WITHOUT ANY WARRANTY; without even the implied warranty of
# MERCHANTABILITY or FITNESS FOR A PARTICULAR PURPOSE.  See the
# GNU General Public License for more details.
#
# You should have received a copy of the GNU General Public License
# along with Foobar.  If not, see <http://www.gnu.org/licenses/>.

timezone:
  $type: group

  name:
    $type: select
    $values: ["CET",
              "CST6CDT",
              "EET",
              "EST",
              "EST5EDT",
              "GMT",
              "GMT+0",
```

```
              "GMT-0",
              "GMT0",
              "Greenwich",
              "HST",
              "MET",
              "MST",
              "MST7MDT",
              "NZ",
              "NZ-CHAT",
              "Navajo",
              "PST8PDT",
              "UCT",
              "UTC",
              "Universal",
              "W-SU",
              "WET",
              "Zulu",
              "Etc/GMT+1",
              "Etc/GMT+2",
              "Etc/GMT+3",
              "Etc/GMT+4",
              "Etc/GMT+5",
              "Etc/GMT+6",
              "Etc/GMT+7",
              "Etc/GMT+8",
              "Etc/GMT+9",
              "Etc/GMT+10",
              "Etc/GMT+11",
              "Etc/GMT+12",
              "Etc/GMT-1",
              "Etc/GMT-2",
              "Etc/GMT-3",
              "Etc/GMT-4",
              "Etc/GMT-5",
              "Etc/GMT-6",
              "Etc/GMT-7",
              "Etc/GMT-8",
              "Etc/GMT-9",
              "Etc/GMT-10",
              "Etc/GMT-11",
              "Etc/GMT-12",
              "Etc/GMT-13",
              "Etc/GMT-14",
              "Etc/GMT",
              "Etc/GMT+0",
              "Etc/GMT-0",
              "Etc/GMT0",
```

```
                "Etc/Greenwich",
                "Etc/UCT",
                "Etc/UTC",
                "Etc/Universal",
                "Etc/Zulu"
                ]
        $default: CET

    hardware_clock_set_to_utc:
        $type: boolean
        $default: True
...
```

`form.yml` contains additional information that describes how the form for a pillar should look for SUSE Manager. This information is contained in attributes that always start with a $ sign.

 Important: Ignored Values

All values that start with a $ sign are annotations used to display the UI that users interact with. These annotations are not part of pillar data itself and are handled as metadata.

The following are valid attributes.

**$type**

The most important attribute is the $type attribute. It defines the type of the pillar value and the form-field that is generated. The following represent the currently supported types:

- text

- password

- number

- url

- email

- date

- time

- datetime

- boolean

- color

- select

- group

- hidden-group

 **Note: Text Attribute**

The text attribute is the default and does not need to be specified explicitly.

Many of these values are self-explanatory: `text` will generate a simple text field, `password` a password field and the `color` type will generate a color picker.

The `group` and `hidden-group` types do not generate an editable field and are used to structure form and pillar data. The difference between group and hidden-group is `group` generates a visible border with a heading, and hidden-group shows nothing visually (and is only used to structure pillar data).

**$default**

`$default` allows you to specify a default value that is displayed and used, if no other value is entered.

**$label**

`$label` allows you to specify the name of a value that is shown in the form. If this value is not set, the pillar name is used and capitalized without underscores and dashes.

**$help and $placeholder**

The `$help` and `$placeholder` attributes are used to give a user a better understanding of what the value should be. `$help` defines the message a user sees when hovering over a field and `$placeholder` displays a gray placeholder text in the field. `$placeholder` may only be used with text fields like text, password, email or date. It doesnt make sense to add a placeholder if you also use `$default` as this will hide the placeholder.

**$scope**

`$scope` allows you to specify a hierarchy level at which a value may be edited. Possible values are `system`, `group` and `readonly`.

The default `$scope: system` allows values to be edited at group and system levels. A value can be entered for each system but if no value is entered the system will fall back to the group default.

If using `$scope: group`, a value may only be edited for a group. On the system level you will be able to see the value, but not edit it.

The `$scope: readonly` option makes a field read-only. It can be used to show a user data which should be known, but should not be editable. This option only makes sense in combination with the $default attribute.

**$visibleIf**

`$visibleIf` allows you to show a field or group if a simple condition is met. A condition always looks similar to the following example:

```
some_group$another_group$my_checkbox == true
```

The left part of the above statement is the path to another value, and groups are separated by `$` signs. The middle section of the command should be either `==` for a value to be equal or `!=` for values that should be not equal. The last field in the statement can be any value which a field should have or not have.

The field with this attribute associated with it will now be shown only when the condition is met. In this example the field will be shown only if `my_checkbox` is checked. The ability to use conditional statements is not limited to check boxes. It may also be used to check values of select-fields, text-fields etc.

A check box should be structured like the following example:

```
some_group:
  $type: group

  another_group:
    $type: group

      my_checkbox:
        $type: boolean
```

By using multiple groups with the attribute, you can allow a user to select an option and show a completely different form, dependant upon the selected value.

 Note: Hidden Values

Values from hidden fields may be merged into the pillar data and sent to the minion. A formula must check the condition again and use the appropriate data. For example:

```
show_option:
```

```
      $type: checkbox
some_text:
    $visibleIf: show_option == true
```

```
{% if pillar.show_option %}
do_something:
    with: {{ pillar.some_text }}
{% endif %}
```

**$values**

$values can only be used together with $type: select to specify the different options in the select-field. $values must be a list of possible values to select. For example:

```
select_something:
    $type: select
    $values: ["option1", "option2"]
```

Or alternatively:

```
select_something:
    $type: select
    $values:
      - option1
      - option2
```

## 4.5   Writing Salt Formulas

Salt formulas are pre-written Salt states, which may be configured with pillar data. You can parametrize state files using Jinja. Jinja allows you to access pillar data by using the following syntax. (This syntax works best when your uncertain a pillar value exists as it will throw an error):

```
pillar.some.value
```

When you are sure a pillar exists may also use the following syntax:

```
salt['pillar.get']('some:value', 'default value')
```

You may also replace the pillar value with grains (for example, grains.some.value) allowing access to grains.

Using data this way allows you to make a formula configurable. The following code snippet will install a package specified in the pillar `package_name`. For example:

```
install_a_package:
  pkg.installed:
    - name: {{ pillar.package_name }}
```

You may also use more complex constructs such as `if/else` and `for-loops` To provide greater functionality. For Example:

```
{% if pillar.installSomething %}
something:
  pkg.installed
{% else %}
anotherPackage:
  pkg.installed
{% endif %}
```

Another example:

```
{% for service in pillar.services %}
start_{{ service }}:
  service.running:
    - name: {{ service }}
{% endfor %}
```

Jinja also provides other helpful functions. For example, you can iterate over a dictionary:

```
{% for key, value in some_dictionary.items() %}
do_something_with_{{ key }}: {{ value }}
{% endfor %}
```

You may want to have Salt manage your files (for example, configuration files for a program), and you can change these with pillar data. For example, the following snippet shows how you can manage a file using Salt:

```
/etc/my_program/my_program.conf:
  file.managed:
    - source: salt://my_state/files/my_program.conf
    - template: jinja
```

Salt will copy the file *salt-file_roots*/my_state/files/my_program.conf on the salt master to /etc/my_program/my_program.conf on the minion and template it with Jinja. This allows you to use Jinja in the file, exactly like shown above for states:

```
some_config_option = {{ pillar.config_option_a }}
```

## 4.6  Separating Data

It is often a good idea to separate data from a state to increase its flexibility and add re-usability value. This is often done by writing values into a separate file named `map.jinja`. This file should be placed within the same directory as your state files.

The following example will set `data` to a dictionary with different values, depending on which system the state runs on. It will also merge data with the pillar using the `some.pillar.data` value so you can access `some.pillar.data.value` by just using `data.value`.

You can also choose to override defined values from pillars (for example, by overriding `some.pillar.data.package` in the example).

```
{% set data = salt['grains.filter_by']({
    'Suse': {
        'package': 'packageA',
        'service': 'serviceA'
    },
    'RedHat': {
        'package': 'package_a',
        'service': 'service_a'
    }
}, merge=salt['pillar.get']('some:pillar:data')) %}
```

After creating a map file like the above example, you can easily maintain compatibility with multiple system types while accessing "deep" pillar data in a simpler way. Now you can import and use `data` in any file. For example:

```
{% from "some_folder/map.jinja" import data with context %}

install_package_a:
  pkg.installed:
    - name: {{ data.package }}
```

You can also define multiple variables by copying the `{% set ... %}` statement with different values and then merge it with other pillars. For example:

```
{% set server = salt['grains.filter_by']({
    'Suse': {
        'package': 'my-server-pkg'
    }
}, merge=salt['pillar.get']('myFormula:server')) %}
{% set client = salt['grains.filter_by']({
    'Suse': {
```

```
        'package': 'my-client-pkg'
    }
}, merge=salt['pillar.get']('myFormula:client')) %}
```

To import multiple variables, separate them with a comma. For Example:

```
{% from "map.jinja" import server, client with context %}
```

Formulas utilized with SUSE Manager should follow formula conventions listed in the official documentation: https://docs.saltstack.com/en/latest/topics/development/conventions/formulas.html ↗

# 4.7  SUSE Manager Generated Pillar Data

When pillar data is generated (for example, after applying the highstate) the following external pillar script generates pillar data for packages, group ids, etc. and includes all pillar data for a system:

```
/usr/share/susemanager/modules/pillar/suma_minion.py
```

The process is executed as follows:

1. The `suma_minion.py` script starts and finds all formulas for a system (by checking the `group_formulas.json` and `server_formulas.json` files).

2. `suma_minion.py` loads the values for each formula (groups and from the system) and merges them with the highstate (default: if no values are found, a group overrides a system if $scope: group etc.).

3. `suma_minion.py` also includes a list of formulas applied to the system in a pillar named formulas. This structure makes it possible to include states. The top file (in this case specifically generated by the `mgr_master_tops.py` script) includes a state called formulas for each system. This includes the `formulas.sls` file located in:

   ```
   /usr/share/susemanager/formulas/states/
   ```

   The content looks similar to the following:

   ```
   include: {{ pillar["formulas"] }}
   ```

This pillar includes all formulas, that are specified in pillar data generated from the external pillar script.

## 4.8 Formula Requirements

Formulas should be designed/created directly after a SUSE Manager installation, but if you encounter any issues check the following:

- The external pillar script (`suma_minion.py`) must include formula data.

- Data is saved to `/srv/susemanager/formula_data` and the `pillar` and `group_pillar` sub-directories. These should be automatically generated by the server.

- Formulas must be included for every minion listed in the top file. Currently this process is initiated by the `mgr_master_tops.py` script which includes the formulas.sls file located in:

```
/usr/share/susemanager/formulas/states/
```

This directory must be a salt file root. File roots are configured on the salt-master (SUSE Manager) located in:

```
/etc/salt/master.d/susemanager.conf
```

## 4.9 Using Salt Formulas with SUSE Manager

The following procedure provides an overview on using Salt Formulas with SUSE Manager.

1. Official formulas may be installed as RPMs. If you have written your own formulas, place the states within `/srv/salt/your-formula-name/` and the metadata (`form.yml` and `metadata.yml`) in `/srv/formula_metadata/your-formula-name/`. After installing your formulas they will appear in *Salt › Formula Cataolg*.

2. To begin using a formula, apply it to a group or system. Apply a formula to a group or system by selecting the *Formulas* tab of a system's details page or system group. From the *Formulas* page you can select any formulas you wish to apply to a group or system. Click the *Save* button to save your changes to the database.

3. After applying one or more formulas to a group or system, additional tabs will become available from the top menu, one for each formula selected. From these tabs you may configure your formulas.

4. When you have finished customizing your formula values you will need to apply the high-state for them to take effect. Applying the highstate will execute the state associated with the formula and configure targeted systems. You can use the *Apply Highstate* button from any formulas page of a group.

5. When a change to any of your values is required or you need to re-apply the formula state because of a failure or bug, change values located on your formula pages and re-apply the highstate. Salt will ensure that only modified values are adjusted and restart or reinstall services only when necessary.

This conclude your introduction to Salt Formulas. For additional information, see https://docs.saltstack.com/en/latest/topics/development/conventions/formulas.html↗.

# 5 Configuration Management with Salt

## 5.1 Configuration Management Overview

Salt is capable of applying states by matching minions with relevant state data. This data comes from SUSE Manager in the form of package and custom states.

## 5.2 State Data: Levels of Hierarchy

State data comes from SUSE Manager in the form of package and custom states and targets minions at three specific levels of hierarchy. The state hierarchy is defined by the following order or priority: Individual minions have priority on packages and custom states over groups. Next a group has priority over the organization.

- Minion Level

    - *Systems › Specific Minion › States*

- Group Level

    - *Systems › System Groups*

- Organization Level

    - *Systems › Manage System Types: › My Organization*

For example:

- Org1 requires that vim version 1 is installed

- Group1 requires that vim version 2 is installed

- Group2 requires any version installed

This would lead to the following order of hierarchy:

- Minion1 part of [Org1, Group1] wants vim removed, vim is removed (Minion Level)

- Minion2 part of [Org1, Group1] wants vim version 2 gets version 2 (Group Level)

- Minion3 part of [Org1, Group1] wants any version, gets version 2 (Org Level)

- Minion4 part of[Org1, Group2] wants any version, gets vim version 1 (Org Level)

## 5.3 Salt States Storage Locations

The SUSE Manager salt-master reads its state data from three file root locations.

The directory `/usr/share/susemanager/salt` is used by SUSE Manager and comes from the susemanager-sls. It is shipped and updated together with SUSE Manager and includes certificate setup and common state logic to be applied to packages and channels.

The directory `/srv/susemanager/salt` is generated by SUSE Manager and based on assigned channels and packages for minions, groups and organizations. This file will be overwritten and regenerated. This could be thought of as the SUSE Manager database translated into salt directives.

The third directory `/srv/salt` is for custom state data, modules etc. SUSE Manager does not operate within or utilize this directory. However the state data placed here affects the Highstate of minions and is merged with the total state result generated by SUSE Manager.

## 5.4 SUSE Manager States

All sls files created by users will be saved to disk on the salt-master server. These files will be placed in `/srv/susemanager/salt/` and each organization will be placed within its own directory. Although these states are custom, these states are created using SUSE Manager. The following provides an overview of directory structure:

```
├── manager_org_DEVEL
│   ├── files
│   │    ... files needed by states (uploaded by users)...
│   └── state.sls
         ... other sls files (created by users)...
E.g.:
├── manager_org_TESTING
│   ├── files
│   │   └── motd     # user created
│   │   ... other files needed by states ...
│   └── motd.sls    # user created
         ... other sls files ...
```

## 5.5 Pillar Data Exposed by SUSE Manager

SUSE Manager exposes a small amount of internal data like group membership, organization membership and file roots as pillars which can be used with custom sls states. These are managed by SUSE Manager or by the user.

To avoid hard-coding organization id's within sls files, a pillar entry is added for each organization:

```
org-files-dir: relative_path_to_files
```

This file will be available for all minions which belong to this organization.

The following represents a Pillar example located in `/etc/motd`:

```
file.managed:
    - source: salt://{{ pillar['org-files-dir']}}/motd
    - user: root
    - group: root
    - mode: 644
```

# 6 Salt Minion Scalability

## 6.1 Salt Minion Onboarding Rate

The rate at which SUSE Manager can on-board minions (accept Salt keys) is limited and depends on hardware resources. On-boarding minions at a faster rate than SUSE Manager is configured for will build up a backlog of unprocessed keys slowing the process and potentially exhausting resources. It is recommended to limit the acceptance key rate pro-grammatically. A safe starting point would be to on-board a minion every 15 seconds, which can be implemented via the following command:

```
for k in $(salt-key -l un|grep -v Unaccepted); do salt-key -y -a $k; sleep 15; done
```

## 6.2 Minions Running with Unaccepted Salt Keys

Minions which have not been on-boarded, (minions running with unaccepted Salt keys) consume resources, in particular inbound network bandwidth for ~2.5 Kb/s per minion. 1000 idle minions will consume around ~2.5 Mb/s, and this number will drop to almost 0 once on-boarding has been completed. Limit non-onboarded systems for optimal performance.

Salt's official documentation suggests the maximum number of opened files should be set to at least 2 × the minion count. Current default is 16384, which is sufficient for ~8000 minions. For larger installations, this number may be increased by editing the following line in /usr/lib/systemd/system/salt-master.service:

```
LimitNOFILE=16384
```

# 6.3 Salt Timeouts

## 6.3.1 Background Information

Salt features two timeout parameters called `timeout` and `gather_job_timeout` that are relevant during the execution of Salt commands and jobs—it does not matter whether they are triggered using the command line interface or API. These two parameters are explained in the following article.

This is a normal workflow when all minions are well reachable:

- A salt command or job is executed:

```
salt '*' test.ping
```

- Salt master publishes the job with the targeted minions into the Salt PUB channel.

- Minions take that job and start working on it.

- Salt master is looking at the Salt RET channel to gather responses from the minions.

- If Salt master gets all responses from targeted minions, then everything is completed and Salt master will return a response containing all the minion responses.

If some of the minions are down during this process, the workflow continues as follows:

1. If `timeout` is reached before getting all expected responses from the minions, then Salt master would trigger an aditional job (a Salt **find_job** job) targeting only pending minions to check whether the job is already running on the minion.

2. Now `gather_job_timeout` is evaluated. A new counter is now triggered.

3. If this new **find_job** job responses that the original job is actually running on the minion, then Salt master will wait for that minion's response.

4. In case of reaching `gather_job_timeout` without having any response from the minion (neither for the initial **test.ping** nor for the **find_job** job), Salt master will return with only the gathered responses from the responding minions.

By default, SUSE Manager globally sets `timeout` and `gather_job_timeout` to 120 seconds. So, in the worst case, a Salt call targeting unreachable minions will end up *with 240 seconds of waiting* until getting a response.

### 6.3.2   A Presence Ping Mechanism for Unreachable Salt Minions

In order to prevent waiting until timeouts are reached when some minions are down, SUSE introduced a so-called "presence mechanism" for Salt minions.

On SUSE Manager 3.0.5 and later, this presence mechanism checks for unreachable Salt minions when SUSE Manager is performing synchronous calls to these minions, and it excludes unreachable minions from that call. Synchronous calls are going to be displaced in favor of asynchronous calls but currently still being used during some workflows.

The presence mechanism triggers a Salt **test.ping** with a custom and fixed short Salt timeout values. Default Salt values for the presence ping are: `timeout = 4` and `gather_job_timeout = 1`. This way, we can quickly detect which targeted minions are unreachable, and then exclude them from the synchronous call.

### 6.3.3   Overriding Salt Presence Timeout Values

SUSE Manager administrators can increase or decrease default presence ping timeout values by removing the comment markers (`#`) and setting the desired values for `salt_presence_ping_timeout` and `salt_presence_ping_gather_job_timeout` options in `/etc/rhn/rhn.conf`:

```
# SUSE Manager presence timeouts for Salt minions
# salt_presence_ping_timeout = 4
# salt_presence_ping_gather_job_timeout = 1
```

### 6.3.4   Salt SSH Minions (SSH Push)

Salt SSH minions are slightly different that regular minions (zeromq). Salt SSH minions do not use Salt PUB/RET channels but a wrapper Salt command inside of an SSH call. Salt `timeout` and `gather_job_timeout` are not playing a role here.

SUSE Manager defines a timeout for SSH connections in `/etc/rhn/rhn.conf`:

```
# salt_ssh_connect_timeout = 180
```

The presence ping mechanism is also working with SSH minions. In this case, SUSE Manager will use `salt_presence_ping_timeout` to override the default timeout value for SSH connections.

# 7 Activation Key Management

## 7.1 What are Activation Keys?

An `activation key` in SUSE Manager is a group of configuration settings with a label. You can apply all configuration settings associated with an activation key by adding its label as a parameter to a bootstrap script. Under normal operating conditions best practices suggest using an activation key label in combination with a bootstrap script.

An activation key can specify:

- Channel Assignment

- System Types (Traditionally called Add-on Entitlements)

- Contact Method

- Configuration Files

- Packages to be Installed

- System Group Assignment

Activation keys are just a collection of configuration settings which have been given a label name and then added to a bootstrap script. When the bootstrap script is executed all configuration settings associated with the label are applied to the system the script is run on.

## 7.2 Provisioning and Configuration

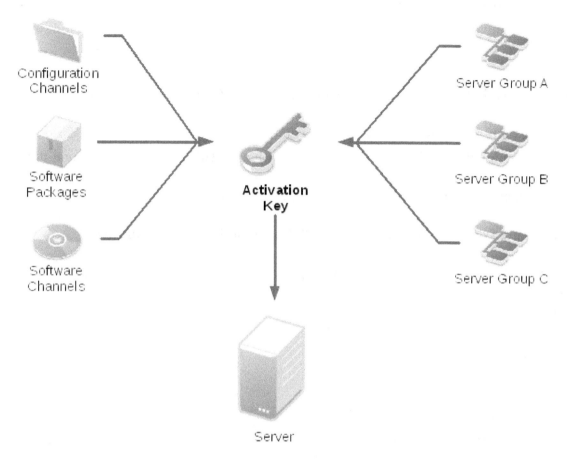

FIGURE 7.1: PROVISIONING AND CONFIGURATION OVERVIEW

## 7.3 Activation Keys Best Practices

There are a few important concepts which should be kept in mind when creating activation keys. The following sections provide insight when creating and naming your activation keys.

### 7.3.1   Key Label Naming

One of the most important things to consider during activation key creation is label naming. Creating names which are associated with your organization's infrastructure will make it easier for you when performing more complex operations. When naming key labels keep the following in mind:

- OS naming (mandatory): Keys should always refer to the OS they provide settings for

- Architecture naming (recommended): Unless your company is running on one architecture only, for example x86_64, then providing labels with an architecture type is a good idea.

- Server type naming: What is, or what will this server be used for?

- Location naming: Where is the server located? Room, building, or department?

- Date naming: Maintenance windows, quarter, etc.

- Custom naming: What naming scheme suits your organizations needs?

Example activation key label names:

```
sles12-sp2-web_server-room_129-x86_64
```

```
sles12-sp2-test_packages-blg_502-room_21-ppc64le
```

### 7.3.2   Channels which will be Included

When creating activation keys you also need to keep in mind which channels (software sources) will be associated with it.

 Important: Default Base Channel

Keys should have a specific base channel assigned to it, for example `SLES12-SP2-Pool-x86_64`. If this is not the case SUSE Manager will be unable to utilize specific stages. Using the default base channel is not recommended and may cause problems.

- Channels to be included:

    - suse-manager-tools

- Typical packages to be included:

    - osad (pushing tasks)

        - Installs `python-jabberpy` and `pyxml` as dependencies

    - `rhncfg-actions` (Remote Command, Configuration Managment)

        - Installs `rhncfg` and `rhncfg-client` as dependencies

## 7.4 Combining Activation Keys

You can combine activation keys when executing the bootstrap script on your clients. Combining keys allows for more control on what is installed on your systems and reduces duplication of keys for large complex environments.

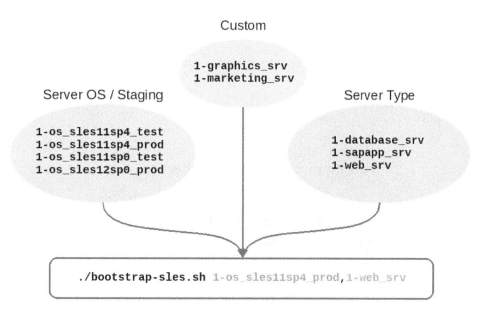

FIGURE 7.2: COMBINING ACTIVATION KEYS

## Combining Activation Keys

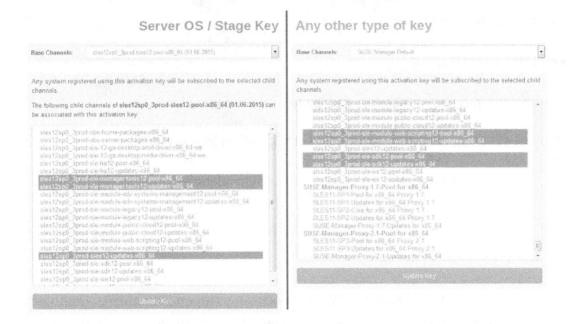

FIGURE 7.3: COMBINING ACTIVATION KEYS 2

## 7.5 Using Activation Keys and Bootstrap with Traditional Clients (Non-Salt)

Create the initial bootstrap script template from the command line on the SUSE Manager server with:

```
# mgr-bootstrap
```

This command will generate the bootstrap script and place them in /srv/www/htdocs/pub/ bootstrap.

Alternatively you may use the Web UI to create your bootstrap script template. For more information, see Book "Reference Manual", Chapter 11 "Admin", Section 11.4.2 "Admin > Manager Configuration > Bootstrap Script".

Use the Web UI to create your keys. From the Web UI proceed to Overview › Tasks › Manage Activation Keys.

## 7.6 Using Activation Keys when Registering salt-minions

With the addition of Salt to SUSE Manager 3 states should now be considered best practice over the more traditional way of combining activation keys. Although states allow for more configuration options you need to place the new system within the correct group so the desired states will be applied to the system. Using an activation key on your minions will place the system within the correct group automatically.

You should be aware of a few facts when working with Salt over traditional activation keys:

- Currently we do not support specifying an activation key on the minion on-boarding page.

- Activation keys used with salt-minions are the same as those used with traditional systems and may be shared.

- The equivalent of specifying a key using the traditional bootstrap method is to place the desired key in the grain of a minion. For more information on grains, see https://docs.salt-stack.com/en/latest/topics/targeting/grains.html ↗

- Once a minion has been accepted either from the *Salt › Keys* page located in the Web UI or from the command line, all configurations specified by the activation key placed within a salt grain will be applied.

- Currently you may only use one activation key when working with salt. You cannot combine them, despite this, salt states allow for even more control.

### 7.6.1 Using an Activation Key and Custom Grains File

Create a custom grains file and place it on the minion here:

```
# /etc/salt/grains
```

Then add the following lines to the grains file replacing 1-sles12-sp2 with your activation key label:

```
susemanager:
  activation_key: 1-sles12-sp2
```

Now restart the minion with:

```
# systemctl restart salt-minion
```

## 7.6.2 Using an Activation Key in the Minion Configuration File

You may also place the activation key grain within the minion configuration file located in:

```
# /etc/salt/minion
```

Now add the following lines to the minion configuration file replacing 1-sles12-sp2 with your activation key label:

```
grains:
  susemanager:
    activation_key: 1-sles12-sp2
```

Reboot the minion with:

```
# systemctl restart salt-minion
```

# 8 Contact Methods

## 8.1 Selecting a Contact Method

SUSE Manager provides several methods for communication between client and server. All commands your SUSE Manager server sends its clients to do will be routed through one of them. Which one you select will depend on your network infrastructure. The following sections provide a starting point for selecting a method which best suits your network environment.

 **Note: Contact Methods and Salt**

This chapter is only relevant for traditional clients as Salt clients (minions) utilize a Salt specific contact method. For general information about Salt clients, see *Book "Getting Started", Chapter 6 "Getting Started with Salt", Section 6.1 "Introduction"*.

## 8.2 Default (the SUSE Manager Daemon rhnsd)

The SUSE Manager daemon ( `rhnsd` ) runs on client systems and periodically connects with SUSE Manager to check for new updates and notifications. The daemon, which runs in the background, is started by `rhnsd.service`. By default, it will check every 4 hours for new actions, therefore it may take some time for your clients to begin updating after actions have been scheduled for them.

To check for updates, `rhnsd` runs the external `mgr_check` program located in `/usr/sbin/`. This is a small application that establishes the network connection to SUSE Manager. The SUSE Manager daemon does not listen on any network ports or talk to the network directly. All network activity is done via the `mgr_check` utility.

 **Warning: Auto accepting (EULAs)**

When new packages or updates are installed on the client via SUSE Manager, any licenses (EULAs) requiring agreement before installation are automatically accepted.

This figure provides an overview of the default `rhnsd` process path. All items left of the `Python XMLRPC server` block represent processes running on a SUSE Manager client.

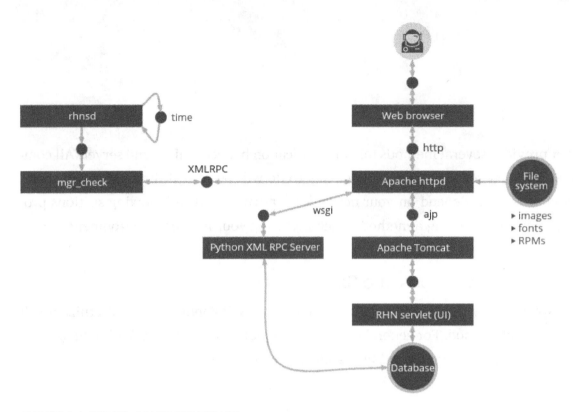

FIGURE 8.1: RHNSD CONTACT METHOD

## 8.2.1  Configuring SUSE Manager rhnsd Daemon

The SUSE Manager daemon can be configured by editing the file on the client:

```
/etc/sysconfig/rhn/rhnsd
```

This is the configuration file the rhnsd initialization script uses. An important parameter for the daemon is its check-in frequency. The default interval time is four hours (240 minutes). If you modify the configuration file, you must as `root` restart the daemon with `systemctl rhnsd restart`.

> ⊝ Important: Minimum Allowed Check-in Parameter
>
> The minimum allowed time interval is one hour (60 minutes). If you set the interval below one hour, it will change back to the default of 4 hours (240 minutes).

## 8.2.2  Viewing rhnsd Daemon Status

You can view the status of rhnsd by typing the command `systemctl status rhnsd` as `root`.

# 8.3 Push via SSH

Push via SSH is intended to be used in environments where your clients cannot reach the SUSE Manager server directly to regularly check in and, for example, fetch package updates.

In detail, this feature enables a SUSE Manager located within an internal network to manage clients located on a "Demilitarized Zone" (DMZ) outside of the firewall protected network. Due to security reasons, no system on a DMZ is authorized to open a connection to the internal network and therefore your SUSE Manager server. The solution is to configure Push via SSH which utilizes an encrypted tunnel from your SUSE Manager server on the internal network to the clients located on the DMZ. After all actions/events are executed, the tunnel is closed. The server will contact the clients in regular intervals (using SSH) to check in and perform all actions and events.

> **❗ Important: Push via SSH Unsupported Actions**
>
> Certain actions are currently not supported on scheduled clients which are managed via Push via SSH. This includes re-installation of systems using the provisioning module. Additionally, image deployments using SUSE Studio will work only when the vhost is permitted to directly connect to the SUSE Studio image store and download the required images.

The following figure provides an overview of the Push via SSH process path. All items left of the `Taskomatic` block represent processes running on a SUSE Manager client.

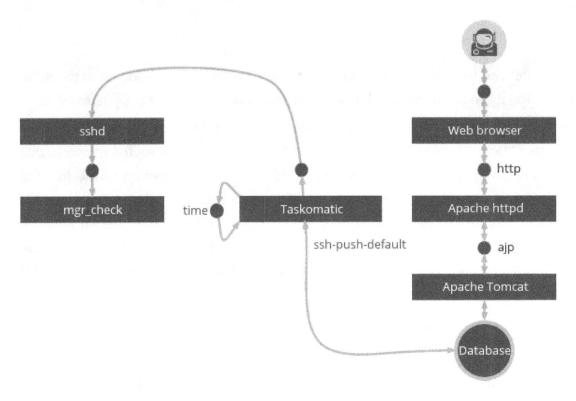

FIGURE 8.2: PUSH VIA SSH CONTACT METHOD

## 8.3.1  Configuring the Server for Push via SSH

For tunneling connections via SSH, two available port numbers are required, one for tunneling HTTP and the second for tunneling via HTTPS (HTTP is only necessary during the registration process). The port numbers used by default are 1232 and 1233. To overwrite these, add two custom port numbers greater than 1024 to /etc/rhn/rhn.conf like this:

```
ssh_push_port_http = high port 1
ssh_push_port_https = high port 2
```

If you would like your clients to be contacted via their hostnames instead of an IP address, set the following option:

```
ssh_push_use_hostname = true
```

It is also possible to adjust the number of threads to use for opening client connections in parallel. By default two parallel threads are used. Set taskomatic.ssh_push_workers in /etc/rhn/rhn.conf like this:

```
taskomatic.ssh_push_workers = number
```

## 8.3.2 Using sudo with Push via SSH

For security reasons you may desire to use sudo and SSH into a system as a user other than `root`. The following procedure will guide you through configuring sudo for use with Push via SSH.

 Note: sudo Requirements

The packages `spacewalk-taskomatic >= 2.1.165.19` and `spacewalk-certs-tools => 2.1.6.7` are required for using sudo with Push via SSH.

PROCEDURE 8.1: CONFIGURING SUDO

1. Set the following parameter on the server located in `/etc/rhn/rhn.conf`.

   ```
   ssh_push_sudo_user = user
   ```

   The server will use sudo to ssh as the configured *user*.

2. You must create the user specified in *Step 1* on each of your clients and the following parameters should be commented out within each client's `/etc/sudoers` file:

   ```
   #Defaults targetpw   # ask for the password of the target user i.e. root
   #ALL     ALL=(ALL) ALL   # WARNING! Only use this together with 'Defaults targetpw'!
   ```

3. Add the following lines beneath the `## User privilege specification` section of each client's `/etc/sudoers` file:

   ```
   <user> ALL=(ALL) NOPASSWD:/usr/sbin/mgr_check
   <user> ALL=(ALL) NOPASSWD:/home/<user>/enable.sh
   <user> ALL=(ALL) NOPASSWD:/home/<user>/bootstrap.sh
   ```

4. On each client add the following two lines to the `/home/user/.bashrc` file:

   ```
   PATH=$PATH:/usr/sbin
   export PATH
   ```

### 8.3.3 Client Registration

As your clients cannot reach the server, you will need to register your clients from the server. A tool for performing registration of clients from the server is included with SUSE Manager 3.1 called `mgr-ssh-push-init`. This tool expects a client's hostname or IP address and the path to a valid bootstrap script located in the server's filesystem for registration as parameters.

 **Important: Specifying Ports for Tunneling before Registering Clients**

The ports for tunneling need to be specified before the first client is registered. Clients already registered before changing the port numbers must be registered again, otherwise the server will not be able to contact them anymore.

 **Note: `mgr-ssh-push-init` Disables rhnsd**

The `mgr-ssh-push-init` command disables the `rhnsd` daemon which normally checks for updates every 4 hours. Because your clients cannot reach the server without using the Push via SSH contact method, the `rhnsd` daemon is disabled.

For registration of systems which should be managed via the Push via SSH tunnel contact method, it is required to use an activation key that is configured to use this method. Normal `Push via SSH` is unable to reach the server. For managing activation keys, see *Chapter 7, Activation Key Management*.

Run the following command as `root` on the server to register a client:

```
# mgr-ssh-push-init --client client --register \
/srv/www/htdocs/pub/bootstrap/bootstrap_script --tunnel
```

To enable a client to be managed using Push via SSH (without tunneling), the same script may be used. Registration is optional since it can also be done from within the client in this case. `mgr-ssh-push-init` will also automatically generate the necessary SSH key pair if it does not yet exist on the server:

```
# mgr-ssh-push-init --client client --register bootstrap_script
```

When using the Push via SSH tunnel contact method, the client is configured to connect SUSE Manager via the high ports mentioned above (see `/etc/sysconfig/rhn/up2date`). Tools like **rhn_check** and **zypper** will need an active SSH session with the proper port forwarding options in order to access the SUSE Manager API. To verify the Push via SSH tunnel connection manually, run the following command on the SUSE Manager server:

```
# ssh -i /root/.ssh/id_susemanager -R high port: susemanager :443 client zypper ref
```

### 8.3.4 API Support for Push via SSH

The contact method to be used for managing a server can also be modified via the API. The following example code (python) shows how to set a system's contact method to `ssh-push`. Valid values are:

- `default` (pull)

- `ssh-push`

- `ssh-push-tunnel`

```
client = xmlrpclib.Server(SUMA_HOST + "/rpc/api", verbose=0)
key = client.auth.login(SUMA_LOGIN, SUMA_PASSWORD)
client.system.setDetails(key, 1000012345, {'contact_method' : 'ssh-push'})
```

 Note: Migration and Management via Push via SSH

When a system should be migrated and managed using Push via SSH, it requires setup using the `mgr-ssh-push-init` script before the server can connect via SSH. This separate command requires human interaction to install the server's SSH key onto the managed client (`root` password). The following procedure illustrates how to migrate an already registered system:

PROCEDURE 8.2: MIGRATING REGISTERED SYSTEMS

1. Setup the client using the `mgr-ssh-push-init` script (without `--register`).

2. Change the client's contact method to `ssh-push` or `ssh-push-tunnel` respectively (via API or Web UI).

Existing activation keys can also be edited via API to use the Push via SSH contact method for clients registered with these keys:

```
client.activationkey.setDetails(key, '1-mykey', {'contact_method' : 'ssh-push'})
```

### 8.3.5   Proxy Support with Push via SSH

It is possible to use Push via SSH to manage systems that are connected to the SUSE Manager server via a proxy. To register a system, run `mgr-ssh-push-init` on the proxy system for each client you wish to register. Update your proxy with the latest packages to ensure the registration tool is available. It is necessary to copy the ssh key to your proxy. This can be achieved by executing the following command from the server:

```
root # mgr-ssh-push-init --client proxy
```

## 8.4   Push via Salt SSH

Push via Salt SSH is intended to be used in environments where your Salt clients cannot reach the SUSE Manager server directly to regularly checking in and, for example, fetch package updates.

 **Note: Push via SSH**

This feature is not related to Push via SSH for the traditional clients. For Push via SSH, see *Section 8.3, "Push via SSH"*.

## 8.4.1 Overview

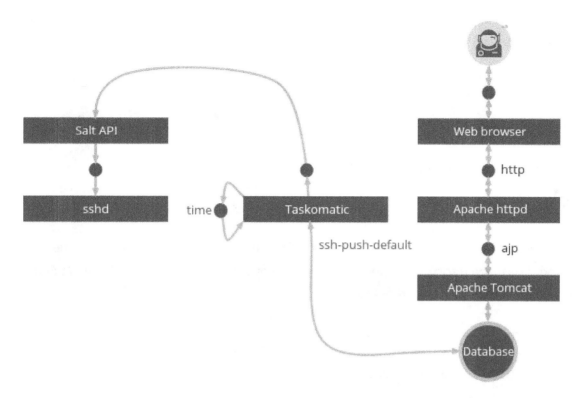

FIGURE 8.3: PUSH VIA SALT SSH CONTACT METHOD

Salt provides "Salt SSH" (`salt-ssh`), a feature to manage clients from a server. It works without installing Salt related software on clients. Using Salt SSH there is no need to have minions connected to the Salt master. Using this as a SUSE Manager connect method, this feature provides similar functionality for Salt clients as the traditional Push via SSH feature for traditional clients. This feature allows:

- Managing Salt entitled systems with the Push via SSH contact method using Salt SSH.

- Bootstrapping such systems.

## 8.4.2 Requirements

- SSH daemon must be running on the remote system and reachable by the `salt-api` daemon (typically running on the SUSE Manager server).

- Python must be available on the remote system (Python must be supported by the installed Salt). Currently: python 2.6.

Note: Unsupported Systems

Red Hat Enterprise Linux and CentOS versions < = 5 are not supported because they do not have Python 2.6 by default.

## 8.4.3 Bootstrapping

To bootstrap a Salt SSH system, proceed as follows:

1. Open the *Bootstrap Minions* dialog in the Web UI (*Systems › Bootstrapping*).

2. Fill out the required fields. Select an *Activation Key* with the *Push via SSH* contact method configured. For more information about activation keys, see *Book "Reference Manual", Chapter 2 "Systems", Section 2.9 "Activation Keys"*.

3. Check the *Manage system completely via SSH* option.

4. Confirm with clicking the *Bootstrap* button.

Now the system will be bootstrapped and registered in SUSE Manager. If done successfully, it will appear in the *Systems* list.

## 8.4.4   Configuration

There are two kinds of parameters for Push via Salt SSH:

- Bootstrap-time parameters — configured in the *Bootstrapping* page:

  - Host

  - Activation key

  - Password — used only for bootstrapping, not saved anywhere; all future SSH sessions are authorized via a key/certificate pair

- Persistent parameters — configured SUSE Manager-wide:

  - sudo user — same as in *Section 8.3.2, "Using sudo with Push via SSH"*.

## 8.4.5   Action Execution

The Push via Salt SSH feature uses a taskomatic job to execute scheduled actions using **salt-ssh**. The taskomatic job periodically checks for scheduled actions and executes them. While on traditional clients with SSH push configured only **rhn_check** is executed via SSH, the Salt SSH push job executes a complete **salt-ssh** call based on the scheduled action.

## 8.4.6   Known Limitation

- OpenSCAP auditing is not available on Salt SSH minions.

- Beacons do not work with Salt SSH.

  - Installing a package on a system using **zypper** will not invoke the package refresh.

  - Virtual Host functions (for example, a host to guests) will not work if the virtual host system is Salt SSH-based.

## 8.4.7   For More Information

For more information, see

- https://wiki.microfocus.com/index.php/SUSE_Manager/SaltSSHServerPush ↗

- https://docs.saltstack.com/en/latest/topics/ssh/ ↗

## 8.5  osad

The default contact method between SUSE Manager and its clients is `rhnsd`. When using the `rhnsd` daemon the client will contact the server every 4 hours and then execute a scheduled action on clients. Depending on your network environment `rhnsd` may not suit your requirements. Alternatively, you may configure `osad` for use with registered client systems enabling immediate execution of scheduled actions. `osad` consists of three components:

**osad.**  A client-side service that responds to pings and runs **mgr_check** when directed by the `osa-dispatcher` running on SUSE Manager.

**osa-dispatcher.**  A service running on SUSE Manager that checks the database to determine if a client running `osad` needs to be pinged or is required to run **mgr_check**, then sends a message telling the client to do so.

**jabberd.**  A daemon that runs on SUSE Manager and uses the XMPP protocol. `osad` and `osa-dispatcher` both connect to this daemon. `jabberd` also handles authentication when using `osad`.

The following figure represents the osad contact method. All items left of the `osa-dispatcher` block represent running processes on the client.

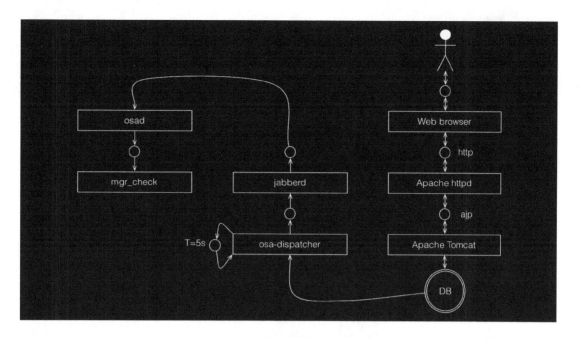

HOW IT WORKS

- On SUSE Manager the `osa-dispatcher` periodically runs a query which checks to see if there are any clients overdue for a ping.

- If an overdue client is found, a message is sent via `jabberd` to the `osad` instances running on all clients registered with your SUSE Manager server. The `osad` instances respond to the ping through the `jabberd` deamon running in the background on your SUSE Manager Server. `osa-dispatcher` receives the response, and marks the client as 'online'.

- If `osa-dispatcher` fails to receive a response from an `osad` instance in a certain amount of time, the client is marked 'offline'.

- `osa-dispatcher` also periodically executes a select on the database to check all SUSE Manager clients which have actions that need to be executed. If an action is found, a message is sent through `jabberd` to `osad` which then executes **mgr_check** on the client. **mgr_check** then takes over performing the actual action.

## 8.5.1  Configuring and Enabling osad

The following procedure enables use of `osad` with SUSE Manager.

## Important: Enabling SSL

For this communication method to work SSL is mandatory. If SSL certificates are not available, the daemon on your client systems will fail to connect. Make sure your firewall rules are set to allow for the required ports. For more information, see *Table 1.1, "Required Server Ports"*.

**PROCEDURE 8.3: ENABLING OSA-DISPATCHER ON SUSE MANAGER AND OSAD ON CLIENTS**

1. On your SUSE Manager server use the following command as `root` to start the `osa-dispatcher` service:

   ```
   systemctl start osa-dispatcher
   ```

2. Install the `osad` package on all client systems allowing communication to the osa-dispatcher on SUSE Manager. The package can be found in the Tools child channel. For more information about child channels, see *Book "Reference Manual", Chapter 6 "Software" Child Channels*.

   ## Warning: osad conflicts with osa-dispatcher

   Do *not* install the `osad` client package on your SUSE Manager server. The `osad` client service conflicts with `osa-dispatcher` server package.

3. When `osad` has been installed, start the service on your client systems. As `root` enter:

   ```
   systemctl start osad
   ```

   Like other services, osa-dispatcher and osad accept `stop`, `restart`, and `status` commands as well.

This feature depends on the client systems recognizing the fully qualified domain name (FQDN) of SUSE Manager. The client systems use this name and not the IP address of the server when configuring the YaST Online Update.

Now when you schedule actions from SUSE Manager on any of the osad enabled systems, the task will be carried out immediately rather than after a client checks in using `rhnsd`.

## 8.5.2   osad Configuration and Logging Files

Each component of `osad` is configured via local configuration files. Changing default parameters is not recommended. For reference the configuration files and logs are found in the following locations.

**osa-dispatcher.**   `osa-dispatcher` is configured via the `rhn.conf` file located on the SUSE Manager at:

```
/etc/rhn/rhn.conf
```

All parameters for configuring osa-dispatcher are located under this section heading:

```
# OSA configuration #
```

**osad.**   `osad` configuration files are located on all SUSE Manager clients at:

```
/etc/sysconfig/rhn/osad.conf
/etc/syseconfig/rhn/up2date
```

For troubleshooting `osad` the log file is located in:

```
/var/log/osad
```

The location of this log file is configurable via the `osad.conf` file.

**jabberd.**   Configuration of `jabberd` goes beyond the scope of this document. The `jabberd` log file is located at:

```
/var/log/messages
```

# 9 Advanced Patch Lifecycle Management

Keeping systems patched and secure remains one of the greatest ongoing challenges that you will face as an administrator. Both proprietary and open-source companies are constantly working to provide updates which fix flaws discovered within their software products.

For the official *Best Practice Guide* on "Advanced Patch Lifecycle Management", see https://www.suse.com/documentation/suse-best-practices/susemanager/data/susemanager.html ↗.

# 10 Live Patching with SUSE Manager

## 10.1 Introduction

Under normal circumstances a system needs to be rebooted after a kernel update. SLE Live Patching allows you skipping the reboot by applying a subset of Linux kernel releases injected via kGraft live patching technology.

In the following sections you will learn how to use SLE Live Patching to avoid the typical reboot requirement after updating a system kernel.

For in depth information covering kGraft use, see https://www.suse.com/documentation/sles-12/singlehtml/book_sle_admin/book_sle_admin.html#cha.kgraft↗.

## 10.2 Initial Setup Requirements

To work with SLE Live Patching the following expectations are assumed:

- SUSE Manager 3.0 or later fully updated.

- At least 1 Salt Minion running SLES 12 SP1 or later and registered with SUSE Manager.

- The matching SLES 12 SPx channels including the SLE Live Patching child channel fully synced.

## 10.3 Live Patching Setup

1. Subscribe all systems to be managed via live patching to your fully synced live patching child channels within your systems base channel by browsing to *Software › Software Channels*. Select both live patching channels and change subscription.

    Note

   When subscribing to a channel that contains a product, the product package will automatically be installed on traditionaly registered systems and added to the package state on Salt managed systems. For Salt managed systems please apply the highstate to push these changes to your systems.

2. Use the search field listed under *Software* › *Packages* › *Install* to install the latest `kgraft` package to all systems to be managed via live patching.

3. Apply the highstate to enable live patching:

4. Once the highstate has been applied on Salt systems or the package has been installed on traditional systems browse to the systems details page for confirmation that live patching has been enabled. You can check the live patching state listed under the *System Info* › *Kernel* table field:

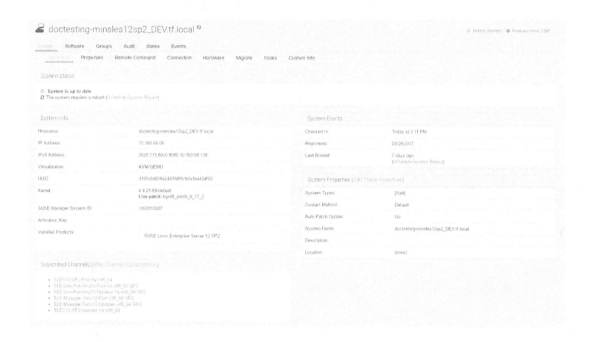

## 10.4  Cloning Channels

It is considered best practice to clone a vendor channel that will be modified into a new channel with one of the following prefix names: (dev, testing, and prod). In the following procedure you will clone the default vendor channel into a new channel named `dev-sles12-sp3-pool-x86_64` using the command line.

1. Open a terminal and as root enter:

```
# spacewalk-manage-channel-lifecycle -list-channels
Spacewalk Username: admin
Spacewalk Password:
Channel tree:

1. sles12-sp3-pool-x86_64
        \__ sle-live-patching12-pool-x86_64-sp3
        \__ sle-live-patching12-updates-x86_64-sp3
        \__ sle-manager-tools12-pool-x86_64-sp3
        \__ sle-manager-tools12-updates-x86_64-sp3
```

```
\__ sles12-sp3-updates-x86_64
```

2. Now use the *-init* argument to automatically create a new development clone of the original vendor channel:

```
spacewalk-manage-channel-lifecycle -init -c sles12-sp3-pool-x86_64
```

## 10.5  Removing Non-live Kernel Patches from the Cloned Channels

In the following procedure you will remove all kernel patch updates located in the dev-sles12-sp3-updates-x86_64 channel that require a reboot.

1. Check the current kernel version in use on your client:

```
# uname -r
3.12.62-60.64.8-default
```

2. From the SUSE Manager WebUI select*Software › Manage Software Channels › Overview › dev-sles12-sp3-updates-x86_64 › Patches › List/Remove*. Type `kernel` in the search field. Find the kernel version that matches the kernel in use on your minion.

3. Remove all kernel update versions that are later than the current kernel.

4. Your channel is now ready to promote for testing SLE Live Patching.

## 10.6  Promoting Channels

The following procedure will guide you through promoting and cloning a development channel to a testing channel. You will change the subscription from the dev repositories on your client to the new testing channel repositories. You will also add the SLE Live Patching child channels to your client.

1. Promote and clone the `dev-sles12-sp3-pool-x86_64` to a new testing channel:

```
root # spacewalk-manage-channel-lifecycle -promote -c dev-sles12-sp3-pool-x86_64
```

2. From the SUSE Manager Web UI under the *Systems* tab select your client system to view the *System Details* page. Select *Software > Software Channels*. From the Software Channels page you can edit which channels a system is subscribed to. Select the new base software channel, in this case it should be `test-sles12-sp3-pool-x86_64`. Click the *Confirm* button to switch the Base Software Channel and finalize it by clicking the *Modify Base Software Channel* button.

3. From the *Software Channels* page select and add both SLE Live Patching child channels by clicking the *Change Subscriptions* button.

## 10.7 Applying Live Patches to a Kernel

The following procedure will guide you through selecting and viewing available CVE Patches (Common Vulnerabilities and Exposures) then applying these kernel updates using the new SLE Live Patching feature.

1. Select your SLES 12 SP3 minion from the *Systems* page to view its *System Details*. Once you have added the SLES 12 SP3 Updates child channel to your client, you should see several `Critical` software updates available. Click on `Critical` to see a list of available patches. Select any of these patches listed with the following synopsis: *Important: Security update for the Linux kernel*. All fixed security bugs will be listed along with their number. For example:(CVE-2016-8666)

    Important: Reboot Icon

   Normal or non-live kernel patches always require a reboot. In SUSE Manager these are represented by a `Reboot Required` icon located next to the `Security` shield icon.

2. You can search for individual CVE's by selecting the *Audit* tab from the navigation menu. Try searching for `CVE-2016-8666`. You will see that the patch is available in the vendor update channel and the systems it applies to will be listed.

**! Important: CVE Availability**

Not all security issues can be fixed by applying a live patch. Some security issues can only be fixed by applying a full kernel update and will required a reboot. The assigned CVE numbers for these issues are not included in live patches. A CVE audit will display this requirement.

# 11 SUSE Manager Server Migration

You can upgrade the underlying operating system and also migrate SUSE Manager server from one patch level to the other (SP migration) or from one version to the next. This works for migrating SUSE Manager server 3.0 to version 3.1.

For migrating from version 2.1 to 3.0, see *Section 11.5, "SUSE Manager Migration from Version 2.1 to Version 3"*.

## 11.1 Service Pack Migration

SUSE Manager utilizes SUSE Linux Enterprise Server 12 as its underlying operating system. Therefore Service Pack migration (for example, from version 12 SP1 to 12 SP3) may be performed in the same way as a typical SLES migration.

 Warning: Upgrading PostgreSQL to Version 9.6 before Migrating to SLES 12 SP3

Before migrating the underlying system to SUSE Linux Enterprise 12 SP3 you must upgrade PostgreSQL to version 9.6.

The migration needs PostgreSQL 9.4 and 9.6 installed in parallel and PostgreSQL 9.4 is only available in SLES 12 SP2. For more information, see *Section 11.2, "Upgrading PostgreSQL to Version 9.6"*.

SUSE offers a graphical and command line tool for upgrading to a new service pack. Comprehensive documentation for executing service pack migration scenarios is located in the SUSE Linux Enterprise Server documentation chapter https://www.suse.com/documentation/sles-12/book_sle_deployment/data/cha_update_sle.html↗.

## 11.2 Upgrading PostgreSQL to Version 9.6

 **Warning: Migrating to SLES 12 SP3**

SUSE Manager Server 3.1 must *not* be migrated to SLES 12 SP3 before upgrading PostgreSQL to version 9.6.

The upgrade needs PostgreSQL 9.4 and 9.6 installed in parallel. PostgreSQL 9.4 is only available in SLES 12 SP2.

Before starting the update, prepare an up-to-date backup of your database.

On existing installations of SUSE Manager Server 3.1 you must run

```
root # /usr/lib/susemanager/bin/pg-migrate.sh
```

to migrate from PostgreSQL 9.4 to version 9.6. During the upgrade your SUSE Manager Server will not be accessible.

The upgrade will create a copy of the database under `/var/lib/pgsql` and thus needs sufficient disk space to hold two copies (9.4 and 9.6) of the database. Because it does a full copy of the database, it also needs considerable time depending on the size of the database and the IO speed of the storage system.

If your system is short on disk space you can do an fast, in-place upgrade by running

```
root # /usr/lib/susemanager/bin/pg-migrate.sh fast
```

The fast upgrade usually only takes minutes and no additional disk space. However, in case of failure you need to restore the database from a backup.

For more information, see https://wiki.microfocus.com/index.php?title=SUSE_Manager/postgresql96 ↗.

## 11.3 Updating SUSE Manager

This section provides information on performing regular updates and running a **spacewalk-schema-upgrade** on your postgresql database.

1. As the `root` user stop Spacewalk services:

```
spacewalk-service stop
```

2. Apply latest patches with:

```
zypper patch
```

3. You will be informed if a new database schema was included in the latest patch. Ensure the database is started with:

```
rcpostgresql start
```

4. Perform the upgrade with:

```
spacewalk-schema-upgrade
```

5. Start Spacewalk services again with:

```
spacewalk-service start
```

 Important: Restart of Services and Applications

Services affected by a package update are not automatically restarted after an update. You need to restart these services manually to avoid potential failures.

You may use **zypper ps** to check for any applications which may be using old code. Restart these applications.

## 11.4 Migrating SUSE Manager version 3.0 to 3.1

The migration can either be done with the Online Migration tool (YaST) or with the Zypper command line tool.

 Note: Reduce Installation Size

When performing the migration, YaST will install all recommended packages. Especially in the case of custom minimal installations, this may increase the installation size of the system significantly.

To change this default behavior and allow only required packages, adjust `/etc/zypp/zypp.conf` and set the following variable:

```
solver.onlyRequires = true
installRecommends=false # or commented
```

This changes the behavior of all package operations, such as the installation of patches or new packages.

## 11.4.1 Using YaST

 Warning: Checking PostgreSQL Version

Before migrating to SLES 12 SP3, check whether PostgreSQL is already updated to version 9.6. For more information, see *Section 11.2, "Upgrading PostgreSQL to Version 9.6"*.

To perform the migration with YaST, use the *Online Migration* tool:

PROCEDURE 11.2: MIGRATING USING YAST

1. If you are logged into a GNOME session running on the machine you are going to update, switch to a text console. Running the update from within a GNOME session is not recommended. This does not apply when being logged in from a remote machine (unless you are running a VNC session with GNOME).

2. Start in YaST *System* › *Online Migration* (**yast2 migration**). YaST will show possible migration targets with detailed summaries.
   In case of trouble, resolve the following issues first:

   a. If the *Online Migration* is not available, install the `yast2-migration` package and its dependencies. Restart YaST, otherwise the newly installed module will not be shown in the control center.

   b. If there are "old" online updates available for installation, the migration tool will warn and ask to install them now before starting the actual migration. It is recommended to install all updates before proceeding.

3. If more than one migration target is available for your system, select one from the list. In case you are still on SUSE Linux Enterprise Server 12 SP1 or SP2, SLES 12 will be upgraded to SP2 or SP3, while selecting *SUSE Manager Server 3.1* as a migration target.

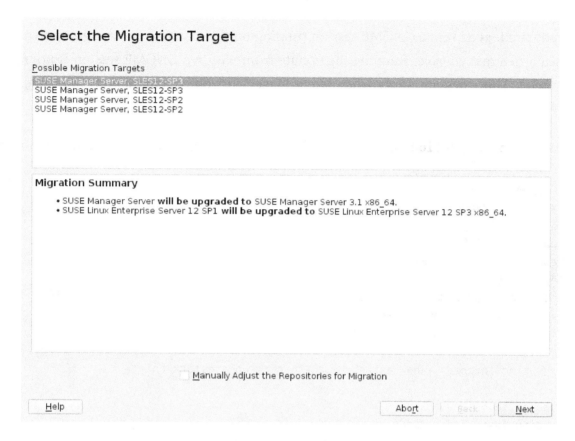

FIGURE 11.1: YAST: SELECT THE MIGRATION TARGET

4. Update the SUSE Manager database schema (`spacewalk-schema-upgrade`).

5. Make sure SUSE Manager is up and running (`spacewalk-service start`).

After finishing the migration procedure SUSE Manager 3.1 on SUSE Linux Enterprise Server 12 (SP2 or) SP3 is available to be used.

## 11.4.2    Using zypper

 ### Warning: Checking PostgreSQL Version

Before migrating to SLES 12 SP3, check whether PostgreSQL is already updated to version 9.6. For more information, see *Section 11.2, "Upgrading PostgreSQL to Version 9.6"*.

To perform the migration with Zypper on the command-line, use the **`zypper migration`** sub-command tool:

PROCEDURE 11.3: MIGRATING USING zypper migration

1. If you are logged into a GNOME session running on the machine you are going to update, switch to a text console. Running the update from within a GNOME session is not recommended. This does not apply when being logged in from a remote machine (unless you are running a VNC session with GNOME).

2. The **`zypper migration`** subcommand show possible migration targets and a summary:

```
# zypper migration
Executing 'zypper  refresh'

Repository 'SLES12-SP1 12.1-0' is up to date.
Repository 'SLES12-SP1-Pool' is up to date.
Repository 'SLES12-SP1-Updates' is up to date.
Repository 'SUSE-Manager-Server-3.0-Pool' is up to date.
Repository 'SUSE-Manager-Server-3.0-Updates' is up to date.
All repositories have been refreshed.

Executing 'zypper  --no-refresh patch-check --updatestack-only'

Loading repository data...
Reading installed packages...
0 patches needed (0 security patches)

Available migrations:

    1 | SUSE Linux Enterprise Server 12 SP3 x86_64
        SUSE Manager Server 3.1 x86_64

    2 | SUSE Linux Enterprise Server 12 SP3 x86_64
        SUSE Manager Server 3.0 x86_64 (already installed)

    3 | SUSE Linux Enterprise Server 12 SP2 x86_64
        SUSE Manager Server 3.1 x86_64

    4 | SUSE Linux Enterprise Server 12 SP2 x86_64
        SUSE Manager Server 3.0 x86_64 (already installed)
```

In case of trouble, resolve the following issues first:

    a. If the `migration` subcommand is not available install the `zypper-migration-plugin` package and its dependencies.

    b. If there are "old" online updates available for installation, the migration tool will warn and ask to install them now before starting the actual migration. It is recommended to install all updates before proceeding.

3. If more than one migration target is available for your system, select one from the list (specify the number). In case you are still on SUSE Linux Enterprise Server 12 SP1 or SP2, SLES 12 will be upgraded to (SP2 or) SP3, while selecting *SUSE Manager Server 3.1* as a migration target.

4. Read the notification and update the SUSE Manager database schema as described (`spacewalk-schema-upgrade`).

5. Make sure SUSE Manager is up and running (`spacewalk-service start`).

After finishing the migration procedure SUSE Manager 3.1 on SUSE Linux Enterprise Server 12 (SP2 or) SP3 is available to be used.

## 11.5  SUSE Manager Migration from Version 2.1 to Version 3

The migration from SUSE Manager 2.1 to SUSE Manager 3 works quite the same as a migration from Red Hat Satellite to SUSE Manager. The migration happens from the original machine to a new one. There is no in-place migration. While this has the drawback that you temporarily need two machines, it also has the advantage that the original machine will remain fully functional in case something goes wrong.

 Important: Migration Process

    The whole process may be tricky, so it is strongly advised that the migration is done by an experienced consultant.

Given the complexity of the product, the migration is an "all-or-nothing" procedure—if something goes wrong you will need to start all over. Error handling is very limited. Nevertheless it should work more or less out of the box if all the steps are carefully executed as documented.

 **Note: Time-Consuming Operation**

The migration involves dumping the whole database on the source machine and restoring it on the target machine. Also all of the channels and packages need to be copied to the new machine, so expect the whole migration to take several hours,

## 11.5.1 Prerequisites

 **Warning: Latest Updates**

The source machine needs to run SUSE Manager 2.1 with all the latest updates applied. Before starting the migration process, make sure that the machine is up to date and all updates have been installed sucessfully.

Only machines running with the embedded PostgreSQL database may be migrated. For the migration of an Oracle based installation, a two-step migration is required: First the installation needs to get migrated from Oracle to PostgreSQL (by means of a separate tool) and afterwards the migration to SUSE Manager 3 can be performed as documented here. As SUSE Manager 3 does no longer support Novell Customer Center but only SCC (SUSE Customer Center), you can migrate a machine only after it has been switched to SCC. The migration script will check if the installation has already been switched to SCC and will terminate if this is not the case. Switch to SCC on the source machine and repeat the migration. During migration the database from the source machine needs to get dumped and this dump needs to be temporarily stored on the target system. The dump gets compressed with **gzip** using the default compression options (maximum compression only yields about 10% of space savings but costs a lot of runtime); so check the disk usage of the database with:

```
# du -sch /var/lib/pgsql/data
```

This will ensure that you have at least 30% of this value available in /var/spacewalk/tmp.

These values from a test migration should aid in illustrating space requirements:

```
suma21:/var/lib/pgsql# du -sch data
```

```
1,8G    data
1,8G    total
suma21:/var/spacewalk/tmp# ls -lh susemanager.dmp.gz
-rw-r--r-- 1 root root 506M Jan 12 14:58 susemanager.dmp.gz
```

This is a small test installation; for bigger installations the ratio might be better (space required for the database dump might be less than 30%). The dump will be written to the directory /var/spacewalk/tmp, the directory will be created if it does not exist yet. If you want the dump to be stored somewhere else, change the definition of the variable $TMPDIR on the beginning of the script to suit your needs.

## 11.5.2   Setup the Target Machine

To prepare the target machine (with the example host name suma30) proceed as follows:

**PROCEDURE 11.4: SETUP TARGET MACHINE**

1. On the target machine install SUSE Linux Enterprise Server 12 SP3 including the extension product "SUSE Manager".

2. Initiate **yast2 susemanager_setup** as you would normally do for an installation of SUSE Manager.
   For more information about installing SUSE Manager, see *Book "Getting Started", Chapter 2 "JeOS Installation"*.

3. On the first SUSE Manager setup screen, ensure that *Migrate a SUSE Manager compatible server* is marked instead of *Set up SUSE Manager from scratch.*

4. On the second screen, enter the name of the source system as *Hostname of source SUSE Manager Server* as well as the domain name. Also enter the database credentials of the source system.

5. On the next screen, you will need to specify the IP address of the SUSE Manager 3 target system. Normally this value should be pre-set to the correct value and you only should need to press Enter . Only in the case of multiple IP addresses you might need to specify the one that should be used during migration.

**Important: Faking the Host Name**

During the migration process, the target system will fake its host name to be the same as the source system, this is necessary as the host name of a SUSE Manager installation is vital and should not be changed once set. Therefore do not be confused when logging in to your systems during migration; they both will present you with the same host name.

6. Continue by following the normal installation steps: Specify the database parameters *using the same database parameters as the source system is recommended.* Enter your SCC credentials. After all the data has been gathered, YaST will terminate.

**Important: Migration Must be Manually Triggered**

The actual migration will not start automatically but needs to be triggered manually. For more information, see *Section 11.5.3, "Performing the Migration"*.

## 11.5.3   Performing the Migration

A migration is performed by excecuting the following command:

```
/usr/lib/susemanager/bin/mgr-setup -m
```

This command reads the data gathered in the previous step, sets up SUSE Manager onto a new target machine and transfers all of the data from the source machine. As several operations need to be performed on the source machine via SSH, you will be prompted once for the root password of the source machine. A temporary SSH key named `migration-key` is created and installed on the source machine, so you need to give the `root` password only once. The temporary SSH key will be deleted after successful migration. Ideally, this is all you will need to do.

Depending on the size of the installation, the actual migration will take up to several hours. Once finished, you will be prompted to shutdown the source machine, re-configure the network of the target machine to use the same IP address and host name as the original machine and restart it. It should now be a fully functional replacement for your previous SUSE Manager 2.1 installation. The following numbers illustrate the runtime for dumping and importing a small database:

```
14:53:37   Dumping remote database to /var/spacewalk/tmp/susemanager.dmp.gz on target
  system. Please wait...
```

```
14:58:14   Database successfully dumped. Size is: 506M
14:58:29   Importing database dump. Please wait...
15:05:11   Database dump successfully imported.
```

For this example dumping the database takes around five minutes to complete. Importing the dump onto the target system will take an additional seven minutes. For big installations this can take up to several hours. You should also account for the time it takes to copy all the package data to the new machine. Depending on your network infrastructure and hardware, this can also take a significant amount of time.

## 11.5.4   Speeding up the Migration

A complete migration can consume a lot of time. This is caused by the amount of data that must be copied. Total migration time can be greatly decreased by eliminating the need to copy data prior to performing the migration (for example, channels, packages, auto-install images, and any additional data). You can gather all data via YaST by running the command **mgr-setup -r**.

Executing **mgr-setup -r** will copy the data from the old server to the new one. This command may be run at any time and your current server will remain fully functional. Once the migration has been initiated only data changed since running **mgr-setup -r** will need to be transferred which will significantly reduces downtime.

On large installations transfering the database (which involves dumping the database onto the source machine and then importing the dump onto the target system) will still take some time. During the database transfer no write operations should occurr therefore the migration script will shutdown running SUSE Manager database services running on the source machine.

## 11.5.5   Packages on External Storage

Some installations may store the package data on external storage (for example, NFS mount on /var/spacewalk/packages). You do not need to copy this data to the new machine. Edit the script located in /usr/lib/susemanager/bin/mgr-setup and remove the respective **rsync** command (located around line 345).

> ⓘ **Important: Mounting External Storage**
>
> Make sure your external storage is mounted on the new machine before starting the system for the first time. Analogue handling for /srv/www/htdocs/pub if appropriate.

In general, all needed files and directories, not copied by the migration tool, should be copied to the new server manually.

## 11.5.6  Troubleshooting a Broken Web UI after Migration

It is possible that the Web UI may break during migration. This behavior is not a bug, but a browser caching issue. The new machine has the same host name and IP address as the old machine. This duplication can confuse some Web browsers. If you experience this issue reload the page. For example, in Firefox pressing the key combination `Ctrl`-`F5` should resume normal functionality.

## 11.5.7  Example Session

This is the output of a typical migration:

```
suma30# /usr/lib/susemanager/bin/mgr-setup -m
  Filesystem type for /var/spacewalk is ext4 - ok.
  Open needed firewall ports...
  Migration needs to execute several commands on the remote machine.
  Please enter the root password of the remote machine.
Password:
  Remote machine is SUSE Manager
  Remote system is already migrated to SCC. Good.
  Shutting down remote spacewalk services...
  Shutting down spacewalk services...
  Stopping Taskomatic...
  Stopped Taskomatic.
  Stopping cobbler daemon: ..done

  Stopping rhn-search...
  Stopped rhn-search.
  Stopping MonitoringScout ...
  [ OK ]
  Stopping Monitoring ...
  [ OK ]
  Shutting down osa-dispatcher: ..done
  Shutting down httpd2 (waiting for all children to terminate) ..done
  Shutting down Tomcat (/usr/share/tomcat6)
  ..done
  Terminating jabberd processes...
        Stopping router ..done
```

```
        Stopping sm ..done
        Stopping c2s ..done
        Stopping s2s ..done
Done.
CREATE ROLE
* Loading answer file: /root/spacewalk-answers.
** Database: Setting up database connection for PostgreSQL backend.
** Database: Populating database.
** Database: Skipping database population.
* Configuring tomcat.
* Setting up users and groups.
** GPG: Initializing GPG and importing key.
* Performing initial configuration.
* Configuring apache SSL virtual host.
** /etc/apache2/vhosts.d/vhost-ssl.conf has been backed up to vhost-ssl.conf-swsave
* Configuring jabberd.
* Creating SSL certificates.
** Skipping SSL certificate generation.
* Deploying configuration files.
* Setting up Cobbler..
* Setting up Salt Master.
11:26:47    Dumping remote database. Please wait...
11:26:50    Database successfully dumped.
Copy remote database dump to local machine...
Delete remote database dump...
11:26:50    Importing database dump. Please wait...
11:28:55    Database dump successfully imported.
Schema upgrade: [susemanager-schema-2.1.50.14-3.2.devel21] -> [susemanager-
schema-3.0.5-5.1.develHead]
  Searching for upgrade path to: [susemanager-schema-3.0.5-5.1]
  Searching for upgrade path to: [susemanager-schema-3.0.5]
  Searching for upgrade path to: [susemanager-schema-3.0]
  Searching for start path:  [susemanager-schema-2.1.50.14-3.2]
  Searching for start path:  [susemanager-schema-2.1.50.14]
  The path: [susemanager-schema-2.1.50.14] -> [susemanager-schema-2.1.50.15] ->
[susemanager-schema-2.1.51] -> [susemanager-schema-3.0]
  Planning to run schema upgrade with dir '/var/log/spacewalk/schema-upgrade/schema-
from-20160112-112856'
  Executing spacewalk-sql, the log is in [/var/log/spacewalk/schema-upgrade/schema-
from-20160112-112856-to-susemanager-schema-3.0.log].
(248/248) apply upgrade [schema-from-20160112-112856/99_9999-upgrade-end.sql]        e-
suse-channels-to-public-channel-family.sql.postgresql]
  The database schema was upgraded to version [susemanager-schema-3.0.5-5.1.develHead].
  Copy files from old SUSE Manager...
  receiving incremental file list
  ./
packages/
```

```
sent 18 bytes  received 66 bytes  168.00 bytes/sec
total size is 0  speedup is 0.00
receiving incremental file list
./
RHN-ORG-TRUSTED-SSL-CERT
res.key
rhn-org-trusted-ssl-cert-1.0-1.noarch.rpm
suse-307E3D54.key
suse-39DB7C82.key
suse-9C800ACA.key
bootstrap/
bootstrap/bootstrap.sh
bootstrap/client-config-overrides.txt
bootstrap/sm-client-tools.rpm

sent 189 bytes  received 66,701 bytes  44,593.33 bytes/sec
total size is 72,427  speedup is 1.08
receiving incremental file list
./
.mtime
lock
web.ss
config/
config/distros.d/
config/images.d/
config/profiles.d/
config/repos.d/
config/systems.d/
kickstarts/
kickstarts/autoyast_sample.xml
loaders/
snippets/
triggers/
triggers/add/
triggers/add/distro/
triggers/add/distro/post/
triggers/add/distro/pre/
triggers/add/profile/
triggers/add/profile/post/
triggers/add/profile/pre/
triggers/add/repo/
triggers/add/repo/post/
triggers/add/repo/pre/
triggers/add/system/
triggers/add/system/post/
triggers/add/system/pre/
```

```
triggers/change/
triggers/delete/
triggers/delete/distro/
triggers/delete/distro/post/
triggers/delete/distro/pre/
triggers/delete/profile/
triggers/delete/profile/post/
triggers/delete/profile/pre/
triggers/delete/repo/
triggers/delete/repo/post/
triggers/delete/repo/pre/
triggers/delete/system/
triggers/delete/system/post/
triggers/delete/system/pre/
triggers/install/
triggers/install/post/
triggers/install/pre/
triggers/sync/
triggers/sync/post/
triggers/sync/pre/

sent 262 bytes   received 3,446 bytes   7,416.00 bytes/sec
total size is 70,742   speedup is 19.08
receiving incremental file list
kickstarts/
kickstarts/snippets/
kickstarts/snippets/default_motd
kickstarts/snippets/keep_system_id
kickstarts/snippets/post_delete_system
kickstarts/snippets/post_reactivation_key
kickstarts/snippets/redhat_register
kickstarts/snippets/sles_no_signature_checks
kickstarts/snippets/sles_register
kickstarts/snippets/sles_register_script
kickstarts/snippets/wait_for_networkmanager_script
kickstarts/upload/
kickstarts/wizard/

sent 324 bytes   received 1,063 bytes   2,774.00 bytes/sec
total size is 12,133   speedup is 8.75
receiving incremental file list
ssl-build/
ssl-build/RHN-ORG-PRIVATE-SSL-KEY
ssl-build/RHN-ORG-TRUSTED-SSL-CERT
ssl-build/index.txt
ssl-build/index.txt.attr
ssl-build/latest.txt
```

```
ssl-build/rhn-ca-openssl.cnf
ssl-build/rhn-ca-openssl.cnf.1
ssl-build/rhn-org-trusted-ssl-cert-1.0-1.noarch.rpm
ssl-build/rhn-org-trusted-ssl-cert-1.0-1.src.rpm
ssl-build/serial
ssl-build/d248/
ssl-build/d248/latest.txt
ssl-build/d248/rhn-org-httpd-ssl-archive-d248-1.0-1.tar
ssl-build/d248/rhn-org-httpd-ssl-key-pair-d248-1.0-1.noarch.rpm
ssl-build/d248/rhn-org-httpd-ssl-key-pair-d248-1.0-1.src.rpm
ssl-build/d248/rhn-server-openssl.cnf
ssl-build/d248/server.crt
ssl-build/d248/server.csr
ssl-build/d248/server.key
ssl-build/d248/server.pem


sent 380 bytes  received 50,377 bytes  101,514.00 bytes/sec
total size is 90,001  speedup is 1.77
SUSE Manager Database Control. Version 1.5.2
Copyright (c) 2012 by SUSE Linux Products GmbH


INFO: Database configuration has been changed.
INFO: Wrote new general configuration. Backup as /var/lib/pgsql/data/
postgresql.2016-01-12-11-29-42.conf
INFO: Wrote new client auth configuration. Backup as /var/lib/pgsql/data/
pg_hba.2016-01-12-11-29-42.conf
INFO: New configuration has been applied.
Database is online
System check finished


===========================================================================
Migration complete.
Please shut down the old SUSE Manager server now.
Reboot the new server and make sure it uses the same IP address and hostname
as the old SUSE Manager server!

IMPORTANT: Make sure, if applicable, that your external storage is mounted
in the new server as well as the ISO images needed for distributions before
rebooting the new server!
===========================================================================
```

# 12 Client Migration

SUSE Manager supports you with upgrading SLE clients to the latest version or SP (service pack). Upgrading from SLE 12, SLE 12 SP1, or SP2 to SLE 12 SP3 or later (when available) is straight forward. Upgrading from SLE 11 SPx to SLE 12 SP3 or later (when available) requires some additional steps, but can be automated.

## 12.1 Migrating SUSE Linux Enterprise Server 12 or later to version 12 SP3

Existing SUSE Linux Enterprise Server 12 clients (SLE) may be upgraded to SP3 with the *SP Migration* procedure provided by the Web UI. The same applies for other supported products based on SUSE Linux Enterprise 12.

 ### Warning: Synchronizing Target Channels

Before successfully initializing the product migration, you first must make sure that the migration target channels are completely mirrored. For the upgrade to SUSE Linux Enterprise 12 SP3, at least the `SLES12-SP3-Pool` base channel with the `SLE-Manager-Tools12-Pool` child channel for your architecture is required. The matching update channels such as `SLE-Manager-Tools12-Updates` and `SLES12-SP3-Updates` are recommended.

**PROCEDURE 12.1: MIGRATING SUSE LINUX ENTERPRISE 12 CLIENT TO SP3**

1. Direct your browser to the SUSE Manager Web UI where your client is registered, and login.

2. On the *Systems* › *All* page select your client system from the table.

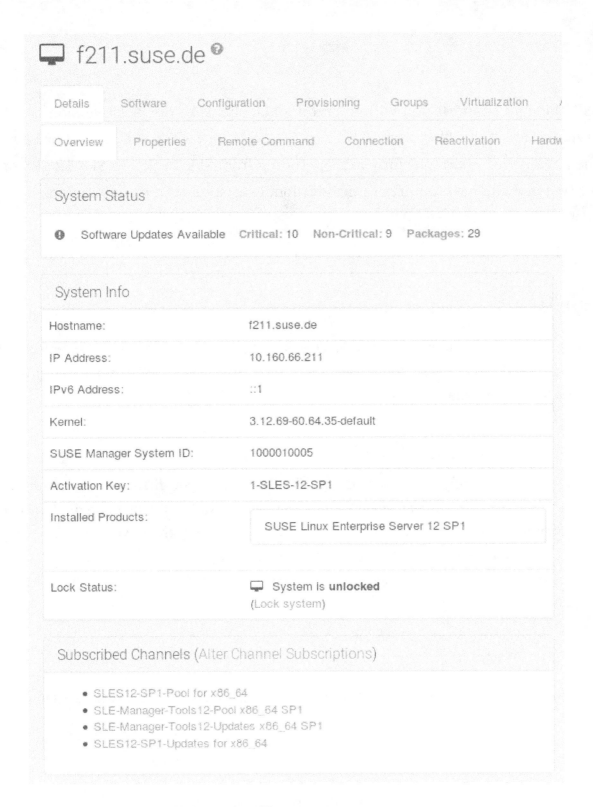

FIGURE 12.1: CLIENT SYSTEM DETAILS PAGE

If there are *Software Updates Available* in the *System Status* notification install these updates first to avoid trouble during the migration process.

3. On the system's detail page (*Figure 12.1, "Client System Details Page"*) select the *Software* tab, then the *SP Migration* tab (*Figure 12.2, "SP Migration Page"*).

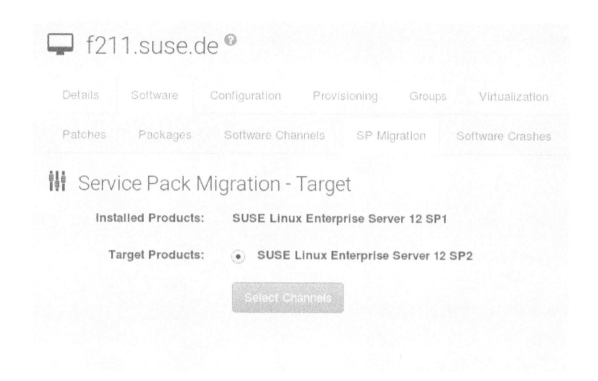

FIGURE 12.2: SP MIGRATION PAGE

4. On *Figure 12.2, "SP Migration Page"* you will see the installed products listed on your client. Select the wanted *Target Products* (if there is more than one), which is SUSE Linux Enterprise Server 12 SP3.

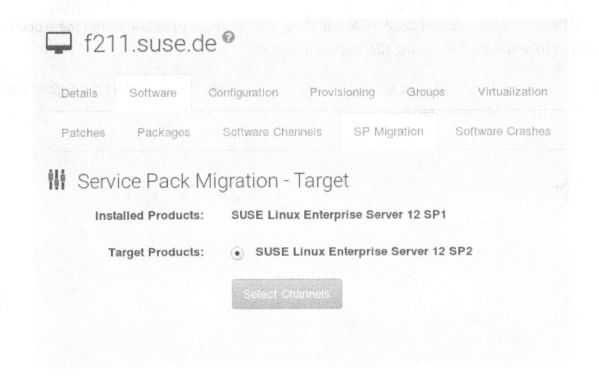

FIGURE 12.3: SP MIGRATION TARGET

Then confirm with *Select Channels*.

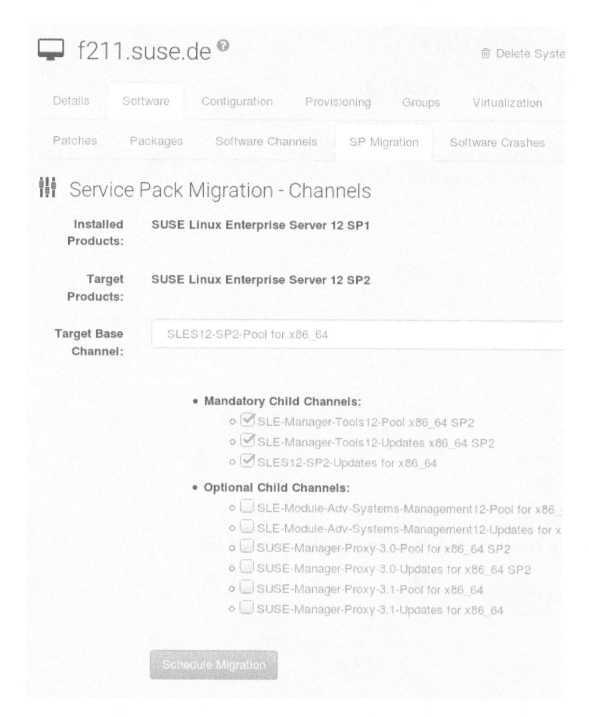

**FIGURE 12.4: SP MIGRATION CHANNELS**

5. **On** *Figure 12.4, "SP Migration Channels"*, ***Schedule Migration,*** **and on** *Figure 12.5, "Schedule Client System Migration"*, ***Confirm.***

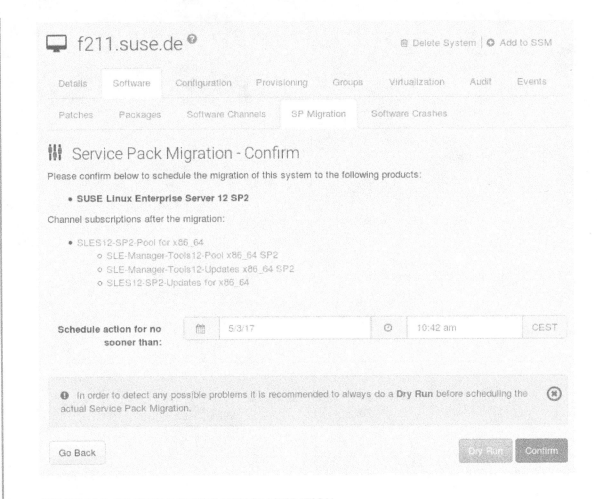

**FIGURE 12.5: SCHEDULE CLIENT SYSTEM MIGRATION**

Check the *System Status* on the system's details when the migration is done.

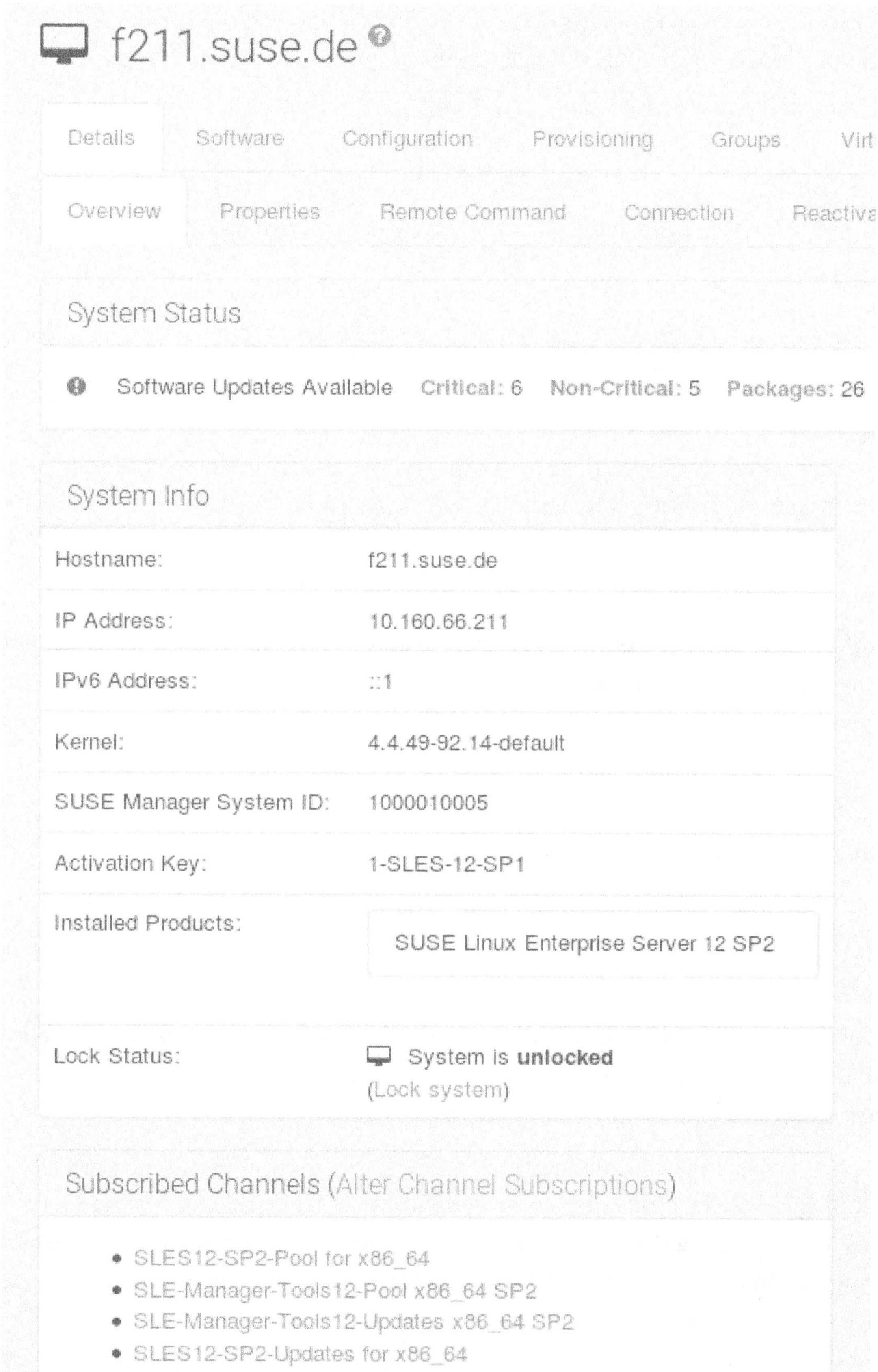

# f211.suse.de ❓

Details    Software    Configuration    Provisioning    Groups    Virt

Overview    Properties    Remote Command    Connection    Reactiva

## System Status

ℹ️  Software Updates Available    Critical: 6    Non-Critical: 5    Packages: 26

## System Info

| | |
|---|---|
| Hostname: | f211.suse.de |
| IP Address: | 10.160.66.211 |
| IPv6 Address: | ::1 |
| Kernel: | 4.4.49-92.14-default |
| SUSE Manager System ID: | 1000010005 |
| Activation Key: | 1-SLES-12-SP1 |
| Installed Products: | SUSE Linux Enterprise Server 12 SP2 |
| Lock Status: | 🖥️ System is **unlocked** (Lock system) |

## Subscribed Channels (Alter Channel Subscriptions)

- SLES12-SP2-Pool for x86_64
- SLE-Manager-Tools12-Pool x86_64 SP2
- SLE-Manager-Tools12-Updates x86_64 SP2
- SLES12-SP2-Updates for x86_64

**FIGURE 12.6: MIGRATED CLIENT SYSTEM**

If the *System Status* notification does not report a successful migration but lists *Software Updates Available*, install the update now and then check again.

Finally, consider to schedule a reboot.

## 12.2 Migrating SUSE Linux Enterprise 11 SP3 to version 12 SP3

SUSE Linux Enterprise 11 SP3 clients may be auto-upgraded to version 12 SP3 by means of YaST auto-installation. The same applies for other supported products based on SUSE Linux Enterprise 11.

During the procedure, the machine reboots and performs the system upgrade. The process is controlled by YaST and AutoYaST, not by plain **zypper** commands.

 Important

> Only perform this migration on client systems managed by SUSE Manager servers. For upgrading the SUSE Manager server itself, see *Chapter 11, SUSE Manager Server Migration*. This is a viable method for major version upgrades such as an upgrade from SUSE Linux Enterprise 11 to 12.

Perform the following steps:

PROCEDURE 12.2: SYSTEM UPGRADE PREPARATION

 Note

> Make sure your SUSE Manager and all the clients you want to upgrade have installed all available updates, including the SUSE Manager tools. This is absolutely necessary, otherwise the system upgrade will fail.

1. On the SUSE Manager server, create a local tree with the SLES 12 SP3 installation sources. This is needed for booting the clients into the installation or upgrade scenario. For example, download the ISO image of the DVD1 with the installation sources and mount the ISO image as `/mnt/sles12-sp3`:

```
mkdir /mnt/sles12-sp3
```

```
mount -o loop DVD1.iso /mnt/sles12-sp3
```

2. Create an auto-installation distribution: For all distributions you want to perform a system upgrade, you need to create a SLE 12 SP3 distribution in SUSE Manager. Use the following steps to create one:

   a. In the SUSE Manager Web interface, click *Systems > Autoinstallation > Distributions*.

   b. Enter a *Distribution Label* for your distribution (for example, use `summer2017`) as a label and specify the *Tree Path*, which is the root directory of the SUSE Linux Enterprise Server 12 SP3 installation sources (for example, in this case `/mnt/sles12-sp3`). As the *Base Channel* use the update target distribution "SLES12-SP3-Pool for x86_64".

   c. Confirm with *Create Autoinstallable Distribution*.

   For more information about Autoinstallation, see *Book "Reference Manual", Chapter 2 "Systems", Section 2.12 "Autoinstallation"*.

3. Create an activation key for your SLE 12 SP3 systems.
   In order to switch from the old SLES 11 base channel to the new SLE 12 SP3 base channel, you need an activation key. Use the following steps to create it:

   a. Go to *Systems > Activation Keys* and click *Create Key*.

   b. Enter a description for your key.

   c. Enter a key or leave it blank to generate an automatic key.

   d. If you want to limit the usage, enter your value in the *Usage* text field.

   e. Select the "SLES12-SP3-Pool for x86_64" base channel.

   f. Decide about *Add-On System Types*.

   g. Click *Create Activation Key*.

   h. Click the *Child Channels* tab and select the required channels. Finish with *Update Key*.

4. Upload an AutoYaST profile.

   a. Create an AutoYaST XML file according to *Section 12.3, "Sample Autoinstallation Script for System Upgrade (SLES 11 SP3 to SLES 12 SP3)"*.

For more information about AutoYaST, see *Book "Reference Manual", Chapter 2 "Systems", Section 2.12.1 "Introduction to AutoYaST"*.

b. Go to *Systems* › *Autoinstallation* and click *Upload Kickstart/Autoyast File*.

c. Paste the XML content in the text area or select the file to upload. Click *Create*.

d. Add `autoupgrade=1` in the *Kernel Options* of the *Details* tab and click *Update*.

e. Switch to the *Variable* tab.

f. Enter in the text field `registration_key=` and the key from *Step 3.b*.

g. Click *Update Variables*.

After you have successfully finished the previous procedure, everything is prepared for an upgrade. To upgrade a system, continue with *Procedure 12.3, "Upgrading SUSE Linux Enterprise Server 11 SP3 to version 12 SP3"*.

**PROCEDURE 12.3: UPGRADING SUSE LINUX ENTERPRISE SERVER 11 SP3 TO VERSION 12 SP3**

 Warning: Synchronizing Target Channels

Before successfully initializing the product migration, make sure that the migration target channels are completely mirrored. For the upgrade to SUSE Linux Enterprise 12 SP3, at least the `SLES12-SP3-Pool` base channel with the `SLE-Manager-Tools12-Pool` child channel for your architecture is required. The matching update channels such as `SLE-Manager-Tools12-Updates` and `SLES12-SP3-Updates` are recommended.

For example, watch progress in `/var/log/rhn/reposync/sles12-sp3-pool-x86_64.log`.

1. Go to the system via *Systems* and click the name of the system. Then on the systems details page, click *Provisioning* › *Autoinstallation* › *Schedule*, and choose the AutoYaST XML profile you have uploaded in *Procedure 12.2, "System Upgrade Preparation", Step 4*.

2. Click *Schedule Autoinstallation and Finish*.
   Next time the machine asks the SUSE Manager server for jobs, it will receive a reinstallation job which fetches kernel and initrd and writes a new `/boot/grub/menu.lst` (containing pointers to the new kernel and initrd).

When the machine boots, it will use the GRUB configuration and boots the new kernel with its initrd. No PXE boot is required for this process. A shutdown of the machine is initiated as well, effectively 3 minutes after the job was fetched.

## 12.3 Sample Autoinstallation Script for System Upgrade (SLES 11 SP3 to SLES 12 SP3)

```
<?xml version="1.0"?>
<!DOCTYPE profile>
<profile xmlns="http://www.suse.com/1.0/yast2ns"
        xmlns:config="http://www.suse.com/1.0/configns">
  <general>
  $SNIPPET('spacewalk/sles_no_signature_checks')
    <mode>
      <confirm config:type="boolean">false</confirm>
    </mode>
  </general>
  <add-on>
    <add_on_products config:type="list">
      <listentry>
        <ask_on_error config:type="boolean">true</ask_on_error>
        <media_url>http://$redhat_management_server/ks/dist/child/sles12-sp3-updates-
x86_64/summer2017</media_url>
        <name>SLES12 SP3 Updates</name>
        <product>SLES12-SP3</product>
        <product_dir>/</product_dir>
      </listentry>
      <listentry>
        <ask_on_error config:type="boolean">true</ask_on_error>
        <media_url>http://$redhat_management_server/ks/dist/child/sle-manager-tools12-
pool-x86_64-sp3/summer2017</media_url>
        <name>SLE12 SP3 Manager Tools Pool</name>
        <product>SLES12-SP3</product>
        <product_dir>/</product_dir>
      </listentry>
      <listentry>
        <ask_on_error config:type="boolean">true</ask_on_error>
        <media_url>http://$redhat_management_server/ks/dist/child/sle-manager-tools12-
updates-x86_64-sp3/summer2017</media_url>
        <name>SLE12 SP3 Manager Tools Updates</name>
        <product>SLES12-SP3</product>
        <product_dir>/</product_dir>
      </listentry>
```

```
  </add_on_products>
 </add-on>
 <upgrade>
  <only_installed_packages config:type="boolean">false</only_installed_packages>
  <stop_on_solver_conflict config:type="boolean">true</stop_on_solver_conflict>
 </upgrade>
 <backup>
  <sysconfig config:type="boolean">true</sysconfig>
  <modified config:type="boolean">true</modified>
  <remove_old config:type="boolean">false</remove_old>
 </backup>
 <networking>
  <keep_install_network config:type="boolean">true</keep_install_network>
  <start_immediately config:type="boolean">true</start_immediately>
 </networking>
  <scripts>
  <init-scripts config:type="list">
    $SNIPPET('spacewalk/sles_register_script')
  </init-scripts>
 </scripts>
</profile>
```

# 13 Postgresql Database Migration

SUSE Manager 3 uses postgresql database version 9.4. postgresql version 9.6 has been officially released for SLES 12 SP3. In the near future postgresql 9.6 will become the base version provided by SUSE Manager. Currently version 9.4 is hardcoded into SUSE Manager, therefore when installing SUSE Manager it will explicitly use this version. This chapter provides guidance on migrating an existing 9.4 database to 9.6 on your SUSE Manager Server.

## 13.1 New SUSE Manager Installations

Once support for postgresql version 9.6 has been officially released for SUSE Manager, no action will be required for new installations. The SUSE Manager extension will pick up the latest version during installation on SLES 12 SP3. This will be fully transparent to the user. Check the active postgresql version with the following command:

```
suse-manager-example-srv:~ # psql --version
psql (PostgreSQL) 9.6.3
```

## 13.2 Migrating an Existing Installation

Before migrating to the new database version, ensure SUSE Manager is fully patched to the latest version. You can check if the system is ready to use postgresql 9.6 by issuing the following command:

```
suma-test-srv:~ # rpm -q smdba
smdba-1.5.8-0.2.3.1.x86_64
```

> **❗ Important**
>
> Postgresql 9.6 requires smdba version 1.5.8 or higher

> **✋ Warning**
>
> Always create a database backup before performing a migration

. The database migration begins by executing the following command:

```
$> /usr/lib/susemanager/bin/pg-migrate.sh
```

The `pg-migrate.sh` script will automatically perform the following operations:

- Stop spacewalk services

- Shut down the running database

- Check if postgresql 9.6 is installed and install it if not already present

- Switch from postgresql 9.4 to postgresql 9.6 as the new default

- Initiates the database migration

- Creates a postgresql configuration file tuned for use by SUSE Manager (The reason for the latest version of smdba)

- Start both the database and spacewalk services

 **Note**

Please note that during the migration the data directory of the database is copied for use by the postgresql 9.6. This results in temporarily doubling the amount of required disk space. In case of a failure, the migration script will attempt a restore to the original state. After a successful migration, you may safely delete the old database directory (renamed to /var/lib/pgsql/data-pg94) to reclaim lost disk space.

## 13.3   Performing a Fast Migration

There are two negative aspects to performing a regular migration:

- You temporarily need double the disk space under `/var/lib/pgsql`

- Depending on the size of the database the migration can take up some time because the whole data directory needs to be copied.

It is possible however to perform a `fast migration`. In this case you do not need the additional disk space as the database files will not be copied but hard linked. This also has the natural effect of greatly increasing the speed of the migration process The entire migration could be completed in less than one minute.

 Warning

Keep in mind if a fast migration fails, database restoration will only be possible with a database backup. Only perform a fast migration if you have an availabel database backup.

Perform a fast migration with the following command (Ensure you have a database backup):

```
$> /usr/lib/susemanager/bin/pg-migrate.sh fast
```

## 13.4   Typical Migration Sample Session

A slow migration should provide you with the following output:

```
d235:~ # /usr/lib/susemanager/bin/pg-migrate.sh
15:58:00    Shut down spacewalk services...
Shutting down spacewalk services...
Done.
15:58:03    Checking postgresql version...
15:58:03    Installing postgresql 9.6...
Dienst 'SUSE_Linux_Enterprise_Server_12_SP2_x86_64' wird aktualisiert.
Dienst 'SUSE_Manager_Server_3.1_x86_64' wird aktualisiert.
Repository-Daten werden geladen...
Installierte Pakete werden gelesen...
Paketabhängigkeiten werden aufgelöst...

Die folgenden 3 NEUEN Pakete werden installiert:
  postgresql96 postgresql96-contrib postgresql96-server

3 neue Pakete zu installieren.
Gesamtgröße des Downloads: 5,7 MiB. Bereits im Cache gespeichert: 0 B. Nach der Operation
 werden zusätzlich 25,3 MiB belegt.
Fortfahren? [j/n/...? zeigt alle Optionen] (j): j
Paket postgresql96-9.6.3-2.4.x86_64 abrufen (1/3),   1,3 MiB (  5,1 MiB entpackt)
Abrufen: postgresql96-9.6.3-2.4.x86_64.rpm [fertig]
Paket postgresql96-server-9.6.3-2.4.x86_64 abrufen (2/3),   3,7 MiB ( 17,9 MiB entpackt)
Abrufen: postgresql96-server-9.6.3-2.4.x86_64.rpm [.fertig]
Paket postgresql96-contrib-9.6.3-2.4.x86_64 abrufen (3/3), 648,9 KiB (  2,2 MiB entpackt)
Abrufen: postgresql96-contrib-9.6.3-2.4.x86_64.rpm [fertig]
Überprüfung auf Dateikonflikte läuft: [......fertig]
(1/3) Installieren: postgresql96-9.6.3-2.4.x86_64 [...........fertig]
(2/3) Installieren: postgresql96-server-9.6.3-2.4.x86_64 [............fertig]
(3/3) Installieren: postgresql96-contrib-9.6.3-2.4.x86_64 [...........fertig]
15:58:08    Ensure postgresql 9.6 is being used as default...
```

```
15:58:09   Successfully switched to new postgresql version 9.6.
15:58:09   Create new database directory...
15:58:09   Initialize new postgresql 9.6 database...
The files belonging to this database system will be owned by user "postgres".
This user must also own the server process.

The database cluster will be initialized with locale "en_US.UTF-8".
The default database encoding has accordingly been set to "UTF8".
The default text search configuration will be set to "english".

Data page checksums are disabled.

fixing permissions on existing directory /var/lib/pgsql/data ... ok
creating subdirectories ... ok
selecting default max_connections ... 100
selecting default shared_buffers ... 128MB
selecting dynamic shared memory implementation ... posix
creating configuration files ... ok
running bootstrap script ... ok
performing post-bootstrap initialization ... ok
syncing data to disk ... ok

WARNING: enabling "trust" authentication for local connections
You can change this by editing pg_hba.conf or using the option -A, or
--auth-local and --auth-host, the next time you run initdb.

Success. You can now start the database server using:

    pg_ctl -D /var/lib/pgsql/data -l logfile start

15:58:12   Successfully initialized new postgresql 9.6 database.
15:58:12   Upgrade database to new version postgresql 9.6...
Performing Consistency Checks
-----------------------------
Checking cluster versions                                ok
Checking database user is the install user               ok
Checking database connection settings                    ok
Checking for prepared transactions                       ok
Checking for reg* system OID user data types             ok
Checking for contrib/isn with bigint-passing mismatch    ok
Checking for roles starting with 'pg_'                   ok
Creating dump of global objects                          ok
Creating dump of database schemas
  postgres
  susemanager
  template1
                                                         ok
```

```
Checking for presence of required libraries                     ok
Checking database user is the install user                      ok
Checking for prepared transactions                              ok


If pg_upgrade fails after this point, you must re-initdb the
new cluster before continuing.


Performing Upgrade
------------------
Analyzing all rows in the new cluster                           ok
Freezing all rows on the new cluster                            ok
Deleting files from new pg_clog                                 ok
Copying old pg_clog to new server                               ok
Setting next transaction ID and epoch for new cluster           ok
Deleting files from new pg_multixact/offsets                    ok
Copying old pg_multixact/offsets to new server                  ok
Deleting files from new pg_multixact/members                    ok
Copying old pg_multixact/members to new server                  ok
Setting next multixact ID and offset for new cluster            ok
Resetting WAL archives                                          ok
Setting frozenxid and minmxid counters in new cluster           ok
Restoring global objects in the new cluster                     ok
Restoring database schemas in the new cluster
  postgres
  susemanager
  template1
                                                                ok
Copying user relation files
  /var/lib/pgsql/data-pg94/base/12753/12710


[...]


  /var/lib/pgsql/data-pg94/base/1/12574

                                                                ok
Setting next OID for new cluster                                ok
Sync data directory to disk                                     ok
Creating script to analyze new cluster                          ok
Creating script to delete old cluster                           ok


Upgrade Complete
----------------
Optimizer statistics are not transferred by pg_upgrade so,
once you start the new server, consider running:
    ./analyze_new_cluster.sh


Running this script will delete the old cluster's data files:
    ./delete_old_cluster.sh
```

```
15:58:51    Successfully upgraded database to postgresql 9.6.
15:58:51    Tune new postgresql configuration...
INFO: Database configuration has been changed.
INFO: Wrote new general configuration. Backup as /var/lib/pgsql/data/
postgresql.2017-07-26-15-58-51.conf
INFO: Wrote new client auth configuration. Backup as /var/lib/pgsql/data/
pg_hba.2017-07-26-15-58-51.conf
INFO: Configuration has been changed, but your database is right now offline.
Database is offline
System check finished
15:58:51    Successfully tuned new postgresql configuration.
15:58:51    Starting spacewalk services...
Starting spacewalk services...
Done.
```

# 14 Database Backup and Restoration

Backing up SUSE Manager can be done in several ways. Regardless of the method chosen, the associated database also needs to be backed up.

## 14.1 Files and Directories Requiring Backup

The following files and directories should be backed up:

- The location of your SUSE Manager database, for example: `/var/spacewalk/db-backup`

- `/etc/sysconfig/rhn/`

- `/etc/rhn/`

- `/etc/sudoers`

- `/srv/www/htdocs/pub/`

- `/var/spacewalk/packages/1` (/2, /3, for each additional organization using custom RPMs)

- `/root/.gnupg/`

- `/root/ssl-build/`

- `/etc/dhcp.conf`

- `/srv/tftpboot/`

- `/etc/cobbler/`

- `/var/lib/cobbler/`

- `/var/lib/rhn/kickstarts/`

- `/srv/www/cobbler`

- `/root/.ssh` (Backup is required when using ssh tunnel or ssh push. Keep in mind if you need to reinstall the server and you do not have a copy of the id-susemanager key saved, you must perform a mgr-ssh-push-init again for all clients.lsls)

- Directories containing your custom data (scripts, kickstart profiles, autoyast, custom rpms, etc) should be included in the backup.

- If you have mountpoints to ISO's needed for distributions, these ISOs and the `/etc/fstab` should be part of your backup.

SUSE recommends backing up the entire `/var/spacewalk/` tree. In case of failure, this will save you lengthy download/resync time. Since `/var/spacewalk/` (more specifically `/var/space-walk/packages/NULL/`) is primarily a duplicate of the package repository, it can be regenerated with **mgr-sync**.

If you are running SUSE Manager in a disconnected setup `/var/spacewalk/` *must* be backed up.

Backing up only these files and directories requires reinstalling the SUSE Manager RPMs and re-registering SUSE Manager. In addition, packages need to be resynchronized using the **mgr-sync** tool. Finally, you have to reinstall the `/root/ssl-build/rhn-org-httpd-ssl-key-pair-MACHINE_NAME-VER-REL.noarch.rpm`.

Another method is to back up all the files and directories mentioned above but reinstall the SUSE Manager without re-registering it. During the installation, cancel or skip the registration and SSL certificate generation sections.

The most comprehensive method is to back up the entire machine. This saves time in download-ing and reinstalling but requires additional disk space and backup time.

 Note

Regardless of the backup method used, when restoring SUSE Manager from a backup, you must run the following command to schedule the recreation of search indexes the next time the **rhn-search** service is started:

```
rcrhn-search cleanindex
```

## 14.2  Administering The SUSE Manager Database with (smdba)

SUSE Manager provides the **smdba** command for managing the installed database.

The **smdba** command works on local databases only, not remote. This utility allows you to do several administrative tasks like backing up and restoring the database, everything from creating, verifying, and restoring backups to obtain the database status and restart the database if necessary. The **smdba** command supports postgres databases.

 Important: Running **smdba** Relies on **sudo** Enablement

Running **smdba** relies on proper **sudo** configuration. **sudo** allows you to invoke **smdba** as a regular user and thus, you are save from executing unwanted system changes.

For example, to allow the user admin (the "administrative UID") to execute **smdba** commands, and thus manipulating the underlying database with the "operative UID", make sure something as follows is configured in /etc/sudoers:

```
admin   ALL=(postgres) /usr/bin/smdba
```

With these settings admin user will be allowed to access the target database account (oracle or postgres).

For configuring **sudo** and its security implications, see the sudo and sudoers manpages and the extensive comments in the /etc/sudoers configuration file.

Find basic information about **smdba** in the smdba manpage.

 Note: Restart Spacewalk Services When Connection is Lost

If you have stopped or restarted the database, Spacewalk services connections may be interrupted. In such a case, execute the following command:

```
spacewalk-service restart
```

## 14.3  Starting and Stopping the Database

There are three commands to start, stop, or retrieve the status of the database. These commands work with both databases. Use the following commands:

```
smdba db-status
Checking database core...        online
```

```
smdba db-stop
Stopping the SUSE Manager database...
Stopping core:          done
```

```
smdba db-status
Checking database core...        offline
```

```
smdba db-start
Starting core...        done
```

## 14.4   Backing up the Database

### smdba

The **smdba** command performs a *continuous archiving backup*.

### Hot Backup

The term hot backup refers to a backup performed when both the database and SUSE Manager are running.

### Cold Backup

The term cold backup refers to a backup performed when both the database and SUSE Manager services are shutdown.

 Important: Database Backup Space Requirements

For both a running/hot database backup or an automated backup of the database using cron you must have at least 3 times the amount of space of the current database. Check current database space usage with **df -h** on /var/lib/pgsql/.

To perform a hot database backup for postgresql, do the following:

PROCEDURE 14.1: PERFORMING A HOT BACKUP

1. Allocate permanent space on your remote storage, which you use for general backups (NAS, iSCSI target, etc.). For example:

```
/var/spacewalk/db-backup
```

Note: Backup on NFS Share

A backup from the SUSE Manager server is not required when the mount point for `/var/spacewalk` is on an NFS share.

This directory should always be the same and never change. It will be a permanent target to store new backups and restore from it during a disaster recovery.

2. Create a directory with the correct permissions in your target directory, e.g., with using **sudo**:

```
sudo -u postgres mkdir /var/spacewalk/db-backup
```

Alternatively, as `root`:

```
install -d -o postgres /var/spacewalk/db-backup
```

Or:

```
mkdir /var/spacewalk/db-backup
chown postgres:postgres /var/spacewalk/db-backup
```

3. If you want to create a backup for the first time, run:

```
smdba backup-hot --enable=on --backup-dir=/var/spacewalk/db-backup
```

This command performs a restart of the postgresql database. If you want to renew the basic backup, use the same command.

4. Perform the hot database backup:

```
smdba backup-hot --backup-dir=/var/spacewalk/db-backup
...
```

If the command exits without any errors, find the backup files in your `/mnt/backup/database` directory.

## Tip: Performing a Cold Backup

When using smdba, you should never require a cold backup. You may perform a cold backup once after initial SUSE Manager installation and configuration. SUSE recommends creating a full-backup once a month or weekly and an additional incremental backup for single days. Moving `/var/spacewalk` to an NFS share that is centrally backed-up, will save you alot of time when a restore is required. The NFS share may also be used during the migration from SUSE Manager 2.1 to SUSE Manager 3.

# 14.5 Automatic Backup with cron

It is important to ensure your SUSE Manager database is backed up within a regularly defined schedule. You can do this with a cron job. The following procedure describes this process.

## Important: Database Backup Space Requirements

For all forms of database backup (hot, cold, or automated via cron) you must have at least 3 times the amount of space of the current database. Check current database space usage with **df -h** on `/var/spacewalk/`.

**PROCEDURE 14.2: AUTOMATIC BACKUP WITH CRON**

1. If you have not created a backup directory do so now:

   ```
   # mkdir /var/spacewalk/db-backup
   ```

2. Set the correct user and rights permissions to the directory:

   ```
   # chown -R postgres:postgres /var/spacewalk/db-backup
   ```

   ```
   # chmod 700 /var/spacewalk/db-backup
   ```

3. Add the following line to the cron job at `/etc/cron.d/db-backup-mgr`:

   ```
   0 2 * * * root /usr/bin/smdba backup-hot --enable=on --backup-dir=/var/spacewalk/db-backup
   ```

## 14.6   Restoring a Database Backup

Use **smdba backup-restore** to restore to an earlier point in time. To restore the backup, proceed as follows:

1. Shutdown the database:

   ```
   smdba db-stop
   ```

2. Start the restore process:

   ```
   smdba backup-restore start
   ```

3. Restart the database:

   ```
   smdba db-start
   ```

4. Run **spacewalk-data-fsck** to check if there are differences between the RPMs and the database.

The above steps can be combined with:

```
smdba backup-restore force
```

In this case it will select the most recent backup and purge the rest. Every time you create a new backup, it also purges the previous backups.

 Note: Restoring the Most Recent Backup Only

Because **smdba** makes automatic running database backups, it allows restoration of only the most recent backup, which includes merging of current archive logs.

## 14.7   Archive Log Settings

In SUSE Manager with an embedded database, archive logging is enabled by default. This feature allows the database management tool **smdba** to perform hot backups.

With archive log enabled, even more data is stored on the hard disk:

- Postgresql maintains a limited number of archive logs. Using the default configuration, approx. 64 files with a size of 16 MiB are stored.

Creating a user and syncing the channels:

- SLES12-SP2-Pool-x86_64

- SLES12-SP2-Updates-x86_64

- SLE-Manager-Tools12-Pool-x86_64-SP2

- SLE-Manager-Tools12-Updates-x86_64-SP2

Postgresql will generate an additional ~1 GB of data. So it is important to think about a backup strategy and create a backups in a regular way.

Archive logs are stored at:

- `/var/lib/pgsql/data/pg_xlog/` (postgresql)

## 14.8 Retrieving an Overview of Occupied Database Space

Database administrators may use the subcommand **space-overview** to get a report about occupied table spaces, for example:

```
smdba space-overview
SUSE Manager Database Control. Version 1.5.2
Copyright (c) 2012 by SUSE Linux Products GmbH


Tablespace  | Size (Mb) | Avail (Mb) | Use %
------------+-----------+------------+------
postgres    | 7         | 49168      | 0.013
susemanager | 776       | 48399      | 1.602
```

The following command is available for Postgresql. For a more detailed report, use the **space-tables** subcommand. It lists the table and its size, for example:

```
smdba space-tables
```

```
SUSE Manager Database Control. Version 1.5.2
Copyright (c) 2012 by SUSE Linux Products GmbH


Table                               | Size
------------------------------------+----------
public.all_primary_keys             | 0 bytes
public.all_tab_columns              | 0 bytes
public.allserverkeywordssincereboot | 0 bytes
public.dblink_pkey_results          | 0 bytes
public.dual                         | 8192 bytes
public.evr_t                        | 0 bytes
public.log                          | 32 kB
...
```

## 14.9  Moving the Database

It is possible to move the database to another location. For example if your database storage space is running low. The following procedure will guide you through moving the database to a new location for use by SUSE Manager.

PROCEDURE 14.3: MOVING THE DATABASE

1.  The default storage location for SUSE Manager is: /var/lib/pgsql/. You would like to move it, for example to: /storage/postgres/. To begin, stop the running database with:

    ```
    # rcpostgresql stop
    ```

    Shutdown running spacewalk services with:

    ```
    # spacewalk-service stop
    ```

2.  Copy the current working directory structure with the following syntax:

    ```
    cp [OPTION]... SOURCE... DIRECTORY
    ```

    using the -a, --archive option. For example:

    ```
    # cp -ar /var/lib/pgsql/ /storage/postgres/
    ```

    This command will copy the contents of /var/lib/pgsql/ to /storage/postgres/pgsql/.

> **! Important**
>
> The contents of the /var/lib/pgsql needs to remain the same or the SUSE Manager database may malfunction. You also should ensure there is enough available disk space.

3. Mount the new database directory with:

```
# mount /storage/postgres/pgsql
```

4. Make sure ownership is `postgres:postgres` and not `root:root` by changing to the new directory and running the following command:

```
/var/lib/pgsql/ # cd /storage/postgres/pgsql/
/storage/postgres/pgsql/ # l
total 8
drwxr-x---  4 postgres postgres   47 Jun  2 14:35 ./
```

5. Add the new database mount location to your servers fstab by editing `etc/fstab`.

6. Start the database with:

```
# rcpostgresql start
```

Start spacewalk-services with:

```
# spacewalk-service start
```

# 14.10  Recovering from a Crashed Root Partition

This section provides guidance on restoring your server after its root partition has crashed. This section assumes you have setup your server similar to the procedure explained in Getting Started guide with separate partitions for the database and for channels mounted at `/var/lib/pgsql` and `/var/spacewalk/`.

**PROCEDURE 14.4: RECOVERING FROM A CRASHED ROOT PARTITION**

1. Start by installing SLES12 SP2 and the SUSE Manager Extension. Do not mount the `/var/spacewalk` and `/var/lib/pgsql` partitions.

2. Once installation of SUSE Manager has completed shutdown services with **space-walk-service shutdown** and the database with **rcpostgresql stop**.

3. Mount your `/var/spacewalk` and `/var/lib/pgsql` partitions and restore the directories listed in section one.

4. Start SUSE Manager services and the database with **spacewalk-services start** and **rcpostgresql start**

5. SUSE Manager should now operate normally without loss of your database or synced channels.

## 14.11 Database Connection Information

The information for connecting to the SUSE Manager database is located in `/etc/rhn/rhn.conf`:

```
db_backend = postgresql
db_user = susemanager
db_password = susemanager
db_name = susemanager
db_host = localhost
db_port = 5432
db_ssl_enabled =
```

# 15 Authentication Against SUSE Manager

## 15.1 Authentication Via PAM

As security measures become increasingly complex, SUSE Manager supports network-based authentication systems via Pluggable Authentication Modules (PAM). PAM is a suite of libraries that allows to integrate SUSE Manager with a centralized authentication mechanism, thus eliminating the need to remember multiple passwords. SUSE Manager supports LDAP, Kerberos, and other network-based authentication systems via PAM. To enable SUSE Manager to use PAM in your organization's authentication infrastructure, follow the steps below.

1. Set up a PAM service file (default location: `/etc/pam.d/susemanager`) then enforce its use by adding the following line to `/etc/rhn/rhn.conf`:

```
pam_auth_service = susemanager
```

    **Note**

   This assumes the PAM service file is named susemanager.

2. To enable a new or existing user to authenticate with PAM, proceed to the *Create User* page and select the checkbox labeled Pluggable Authentication Modules (PAM) positioned below the password and password confirmation fields.

3. To authenticate a SLES system against Kerberos add the following lines to `/etc/pam.d/susemanager`:

```
#%PAM-1.0
auth      include      common-auth
account   include      common-account
password  include      common-password
session   include      common-session
```

    **Note**

   To register a Red Hat Enterprise Linux System against Kerberos add the following lines to `/etc/pam.d/susemanager`

```
#%PAM-1.0
```

```
auth        required     pam_env.so
auth        sufficient   pam_krb5.so no_user_check
auth        required     pam_deny.so
account     required     pam_krb5.so no_user_check
```

4. YaST can now be used to configure PAM, when packages such as yast2-ldap-client and yast2-kerberos-client are installed; for detailed information on configuring PAM, see the SUSE Linux Enterprise Server Security Guide https://www.suse.com/documentation/sles-12/book_security/data/part_auth.html ↗. This example is not limited to Kerberos; it is generic and uses the current server configuration. Note that only network based authentication services are supported.

>  **Important: Changing Passwords**
>
> Changing the password on the SUSE Manager Web interface changes only the local password on the SUSE Manager server. But this password may not be used at all if PAM is enabled for that user. In the above example, for instance, the Kerberos password will not be changed.

## 15.2  Authentication Via eDirectory and PAM

1. First check to ensure eDirectory authentication is working with your current OS for example:

```
#getent passwd
```

2. If users are returned from eDirectory then create the following file:

```
# cat /etc/pam.d/susemanager
```

3. And add the following content:

```
#%PAM-1.0
auth      include     common-auth
account   include     common-account
password  include     common-password
session   include     common-session
#
```

4. Finally add the following lines to the SUSE Manager conf file:

```
# grep -i pam /etc/rhn/rhn.conf
pam_auth_service = susemanager
```

5. You may now create users with the same id that appears on eDirectory and mark the Use PAM check-box from the SUSE Manager WebUI.

# 16 Using a Custom SSL Certificate

The following section will guide you through using a custom certificate with SUSE Manager 3.1 and SUSE Manager Proxy 3.1.

## 16.1 Prerequisites

The following list provides requirements for using a custom certificate.

- A Certificate Authority (CA) SSL public certificate file

- A Web server SSL private key file

- A Web server SSL public certificate file

- Key and Certificate files must be in PEM format

### Important: Hostname and SSL Keys

The hostname of the web server's SSL keys and relevant certificate files must match the hostname of the machine which they will be deployed on.

### Tip: Intermediate Certificates

In case you want to use CAs with intermediate certificates, merge the intermediate and root CA certificates into one file. It is important that the intermediate certificate comes first within the combined file.

## 16.2 Setup

After completing YaST firstboot procedures, export your current environment variables and point them to the correct SSL files to be imported. Running these commands will make the default certificate obsolete after executing the **yast2 susemanager_setup** command. For more information on YaST firstboot, see https://www.suse.com/documentation/suse-manager-3/singlehtml/suse_manager21/book_susemanager_install/book_susemanager_install.html#sec.manager.inst.setup ↗.

1. Export the environment variables and point to the SSL files to be imported:

```
export CA_CERT=path_to_CA_certificate_file
export SERVER_KEY=path_to_web_server_key
export SERVER_CERT=path_to_web_server_certificate
```

2. Execute SUSE Manager setup with

```
yast2 susemanager_setup
```

Proceed with the default setup. Upon reaching the Certificate Setup window during YaST installation, fill in random values, as these will be overridden with the values specified in *Step 1*.

 **Note: Shell Requirements**

Make sure that you execute **yast2 susemanager_setup** from within the same shell the environment variables were exported from.

## 16.3   Using a Custom Certificate with SUSE Manager Proxy 3.1

After completing the installation with yast found in *Book "Advanced Topics", Chapter 2 "SUSE Manager 3.1 Proxy"* continue with a modified *Book "Advanced Topics", Chapter 2 "SUSE Manager 3.1 Proxy", Section 2.2.5 "Running* **configure-proxy.sh**" procedure:

1. Execute **configure-proxy.sh**.

2. When prompted with:

```
Do you want to import existing certificates?
```

Answer with y.

3. Continue by following the script prompts.

# 17 Troubleshooting

## 17.1 Registering Cloned Salt Minions

This chapter provides guidance on registering cloned systems with SUSE Manager. This includes both Salt and Traditional clients. For more information, see https://www.novell.com/support/kb/doc.php?id=7012170 ↗.

**PROCEDURE 17.1: REGISTERING A CLONED SALT MINION WITH SUSE MANAGER**

1. Clone your system (for example using the existing cloning mechanism of your favorite Hypervisor)

    **Note: Quick Tips**

   Each step in this section is performed on the cloned system, this procedure does not manipulate the original system, which will still be registered to SUSE Manager. The cloned virtual machine should have a different UUID from the original (this UUID is generated by your hypervisor) or SUSE Manager will overwrite the original system data with the new one.

2. Make sure your machines have different hostnames and IP addresses, also check that /etc/hosts contains the changes you made and the correct host entries.

3. Stop rhnsd daemon with:

   ```
   # /etc/init.d/rhnsd stop
   ```

   or alternatively:

   ```
   # rcrhnsd stop
   ```

4. Stop osad with:

   ```
   # /etc/init.d/osad stop
   ```

   or alternativly:

   ```
   # rcosad stop
   ```

5. Remove the osad authentication configuration file and the systemid with:

```
# rm -f /etc/sysconfig/rhn/{osad-auth.conf,systemid}
```

The next step you take will depend on the Operating System of the clone.

The following scenario can occur after on-boarding cloned Salt minions. If after accepting all cloned minion keys from the onboarding page and you see only one minion on the System Overview page, this is likely due to these machines being clones of the original and using a duplicate machine-id. Perform the following steps to resolve this conflict based on OS.

PROCEDURE 17.2: SLES 12 REGISTERING SALT CLONES:

- SLES 12: If your machines have the same machine ids then delete the file on each minion and recreate it:

```
# rm /etc/machine-id
# rm /var/lib/dbus/machine-id
# dbus-uuidgen --ensure
# systemd-machine-id-setup
```

PROCEDURE 17.3: SLES 11 REGISTERING SALT CLONES:

- SLES 11: As there is no systemd machine id, generate one from dbus:

```
# rm /var/lib/dbus/machine-id
# dbus-uuidgen --ensure
```

If your machines still have the same minion id then delete the minion_id file on each minion (FQDN will be used when it is regenerated on minion restart):

```
# rm /etc/salt/minion_id
```

Finally delete accepted keys from Onboarding page and system profile from SUSE Manager, and restart the minion with:

```
# systemctl restart salt-minion
```

You should be able to re-register them again, but each minion will use a different '/etc/machine-id' and should now be correctly displayed on the System Overview page.

## 17.2 Registering Cloned Traditional Systems

This section provides guidance on troubleshooting cloned traditional systems registered via bootstrap.

PROCEDURE 17.4: REGISTERING A CLONED SYSTEM WITH SUSE MANAGER (TRADITIONAL SYSTEMS)

1. Clone your system (using your favorite hypervisor.)

    **Note: Quick Tips**

   Each step in this section is performed on the cloned system, this procedure does not manipulate the original system, which will still be registered to SUSE Manager. The cloned virtual machine should have a different UUID from the original (this UUID is generated by your hypervisor) or SUSE Manager will overwrite the original system data with the new one.

2. Change the Hostname and IP addresses, also make sure /etc/hosts contains the changes you made and the correct host entries.

3. Stop rhnsd daemon with:

   ```
   # /etc/init.d/rhnsd stop
   ```

   or alternativly:

   ```
   # rcrhnsd stop
   ```

4. Stop osad with:

   ```
   # /etc/init.d/osad stop
   ```

   or alternativly:

   ```
   # rcosad stop
   ```

5. Remove the osad authentifcation configuration file and the systemid with:

   ```
   # rm -f /etc/sysconfig/rhn/{osad-auth.conf,systemid}
   ```

The next step you take will depend on the Operating System of the clone.

1. Remove the following credential files:

```
# rm  -f /etc/zypp/credentials.d/{SCCcredentials,NCCcredentials}
```

2. Re-run the bootstrap script. You should now see the cloned system in SUSE Manager without overwriting the system it was cloned from.

**PROCEDURE 17.6:** SLES 11 REGISTERING A CLONED TRADITIONAL SYSTEM:

1. Continued from section 1 step 5:

```
# suse_register -E
```

(--erase-local-regdata, Erase all local files created from a previous executed registration. This option make the system look like never registered)

2. Re-run the bootstrap script. You should now see the cloned system in SUSE Manager without overwriting the system it was cloned from.

**PROCEDURE 17.7:** SLES 10 REGISTERING A CLONED TRADITIONAL SYSTEM:

1. Continued from section 1 step 5:

```
# rm -rf /etc/{zmd,zypp}
```

2.
```
# rm -rf /var/lib/zypp/  # iiiii except /var/lib/zypp/db/products/ !!!!!
```

3.
```
# rm -rf /var/lib/zmd/
```

4. Re-run the bootstrap script. You should now see the cloned system in SUSE Manager without overwriting the system it was cloned from.

**PROCEDURE 17.8:** RHEL 5,6 AND 7

1. Continued from section 1 step 5:

```
# rm   -f /etc/NCCcredentials
```

2. Re-run the bootstrap script. You should now see the cloned system in SUSE Manager without overwriting the system it was cloned from.

## 17.3 Typical OSAD/jabberd Challenges

This section provides answers for typical issues regarding OSAD and jabberd.

### 17.3.1 Open File Count Exceeded

SYMPTOMS: OSAD clients cannot contact the SUSE Manager Server, and jabberd requires long periods of time to respond on port 5222.

CAUSE: The number of maximum files that a jabber user can open is lower than the number of connected clients. Each client requires one permanently open TCP connection and each connection requires one file handler. The result is jabberd begins to queue and refuse connections.

CURE: Edit the `/etc/security/limits.conf` to something similar to the following: `jabbersoftnofile<#clients + 100> jabberhardnofile<#clients + 1000>`

This will vary according to your setup. For example in the case of 5000 clients: `jabbersoftnofile5100 jabberhardnofile6000`

Ensure you update the `/etc/jabberd/c2s.xml` max_fds parameter as well. For example: `<max_fds>6000</max_fds>`

EXPLANATION: The soft file limit is the limit of the maximum number of open files for a single process. In SUSE Manager the highest consuming process is c2s, which opens a connection per client. 100 additional files are added, here, to accommodate for any non-connection file that c2s requires to work correctly. The hard limit applies to all processes belonging to the jabber user, and accounts for open files from the router, s2s and sm processes additionally.

### 17.3.2 jabberd Database Corruption

SYMPTOMS: After a disk is full error or a disk crash event, the jabberd database may have become corrupted. jabberd may then fail to start during spacewalk-service start:

```
Starting spacewalk services...
   Initializing jabberd processes...
       Starting router
 done
       Starting sm startproc:  exit status of parent of /usr/bin/sm: 2
 failed
   Terminating jabberd processes...
```

/var/log/messages shows more details:

```
jabberd/sm[31445]: starting up
jabberd/sm[31445]: process id is 31445, written to /var/lib/jabberd/pid/sm.pid
jabberd/sm[31445]: loading 'db' storage module
jabberd/sm[31445]: db: corruption detected! close all jabberd processes and run
 db_recover
jabberd/router[31437]: shutting down
```

CURE : Remove the jabberd database and restart. Jabberd will automatically re-create the database:

```
spacewalk-service stop
rm -Rf /var/lib/jabberd/db/*
spacewalk-service start
```

An alternative approach would be to test another database, but SUSE Manager does not deliver drivers for this:

```
rcosa-dispatcher stop
rcjabberd stop
cd /var/lib/jabberd/db
rm *
cp /usr/share/doc/packages/jabberd/db-setup.sqlite .
sqlite3 sqlite.db < db-setup.sqlite
chown jabber:jabber *
rcjabberd start
rcosa-dispatcher start
```

## 17.3.3   Capturing XMPP Network Data for Debugging Purposes

If you are experiencing bugs regarding OSAD, it can be useful to dump network messages in order to help with debugging. The following procedures provide information on capturing data from both the client and server side.

PROCEDURE 17.9: SERVER SIDE CAPTURE

1. Install the `tcpdump` package on the SUSE Manager Server as root: **`zypper in tcpdump`**

2. Stop the OSA dispatcher and Jabber processes with **`rcosa-dispatcher stop`** and **`rcjabberd stop.`**

3. Start data capture on port 5222: **`tcpdump -s 0 port 5222 -w server_dump.pcap`**

4. Start the OSA dispatcher and Jabber processes: **`rcosa-dispatcher start`** and **`rcjab-berd start`**.

5. Open a second terminal and execute the following commands: **`rcosa-dispatcher start`** and **`rcjabberd start`**.

6. Operate the SUSE Manager server and clients so the bug you formerly experienced is reproduced.

7. One you have finished your capture re-open terminal 1 and stop the capture of data with:
   [CTRL]─[c]

**PROCEDURE 17.10: CLIENT SIDE CAPTURE**

1. Install the tcpdump package on your client as root: **`zypper in tcpdump`**

2. Stop the OSA process: **`rcosad stop`**.

3. Begin data capture on port 5222: **`tcpdump -s 0 port 5222 -w client_client_dump.p-cap`**

4. Open a second terminal and start the OSA process: **`rcosad start`**

5. Operate the SUSE Manager server and clients so the bug you formerly experienced is reproduced.

6. Once you have finished your capture re-open terminal 1 and stop the capture of data with:
   [CTRL]─[c]

## 17.3.4 Engineering Notes: Analyzing Captured Data

This section provides information on analyzing the previously captured data from client and server.

1. Obtain the certificate file from your SUSE Manager server: /etc/pki/spacewalk/jab-berd/server.pem

2. Edit the certificate file removing all lines before `----BEGIN RSA PRIVATE KEY-----`, save it as key.pem

3. Install Wireshark as root with: **`zypper in wireshark`**

4. Open the captured file in wireshark.

5. From *EidtPreferences* select SSL from the left pane.

6. Select RSA keys list: *EditNew*

   - IP Address any

   - Port: 5222

   - Protocol: xmpp

   - Key File: open the key.pem file previously edited.

   - Password: leave blank

   For more information see also:

   - https://wiki.wireshark.org/SSL ↗

   - https://bugs.wireshark.org/bugzilla/show_bug.cgi?id=3444 ↗

## 17.4   RPC Connection Timeout Settings

RPC connection timeouts are configurable on the SUSE Manager server, SUSE Manager Proxy server, and the clients. For example, if package downloads take longer then expected, you can increase timeout values. `spacewalk-proxy restart` should be run after the setting is added or modified.

Set the following variables to a value in seconds specifying how long an RPC connection may take at maximum:

**Server** — `/etc/rhn/rhn.conf`:

```
server.timeout = number
```

**Proxy Server** — `/etc/rhn/rhn.conf`:

```
proxy.timeout = number
```

**SUSE Linux Enterprise Server Clients (using** `zypp-plugin-spacewalk`**)** — `/etc/zypp/zypp.conf`:

```
## Valid values:  [0,3600]
## Default value: 180
```

```
download.transfer_timeout = 180
```

This is the maximum time in seconds that a transfer operation is allowed to take. This is useful for preventing batch jobs from hanging for hours due to slow networks or links going down. If limiting operations to less than a few minutes, you risk aborting perfectly normal operations.

**Red Hat Enterprise Linux Clients (using** `yum-rhn-plugin`**) —** `/etc/yum.conf`:

```
timeout = number
```

# 18 Additional Resources

This chapter contains links to helpful resources.

## 18.1 Learning YAML Syntax for Salt States

Learn how to write states and pillars with YAML.

- https://docs.saltstack.com/en/latest/topics/yaml/index.html ↗
- http://yaml-online-parser.appspot.com/ ↗

## 18.2 Getting Started with Jinja Templates

Learn how to begin writing templates in Jinja

- https://docs.saltstack.com/en/latest/topics/jinja/index.html ↗
- http://jinja.pocoo.org/docs/dev/ ↗

## 18.3 Salt Best Practices

Best practices from the Salt team.

- https://docs.saltstack.com/en/latest/topics/best_practices.html ↗

# 19 A SUSE Manager 2.1 and 3.1 Product Comparison

You may already have experience managing your systems using SUSE Manager 2.1. The good news is all the features you are used to working with, (regarding the traditional stack) have not changed. The only real exception is that the original built-in monitoring feature has been removed. Icinga, a third party monitoring solution is included within the SUSE Manager Tools Channel for SLES12. SUSE Manager 3.1 supports managing systems via the popular IT orchestration engine Salt, in addition to the previously existing traditional management stack.

> **Important: Selecting a Management Method**
>
> You cannot and should not mix a single system with both methods although you can have Salt managed systems and traditionally managed systems coexisting and managed by a SUSE Manager server. You may for example have a development department and assign all machines in this department as Salt minions, likewise you could also have a production department and assign machines as traditional bootstrap clients. Remember a single machine is either traditionally managed or Salt but never both.

Keep in mind that minions are not traditional clients and their feature set is currently limited. Future maintenance updates will provide feature parity over time and your feedback for prioritization of these features is welcome! The following tables provide a comparison between each feature set. This includes features in development and features available only to their parent management stack.

TABLE 19.1: COMPARING TRADITIONAL MANAGEMENT AND SALT MANAGEMENT

| Feature/Function | Traditional Management | Salt Management |
|---|---|---|
| Registration | bootstrap/rhnreg_ks | Accept Minion Keys |
| Install Packages | Supported | Supported |
| Install Patches | Supported | Supported |
| Remote Commands | Supported *Scheduled* | Supported *Real-time* |
| System Package States | Unsupported | Supported |
| System Custom States | Unsupported | Supported |

| Feature/Function | Traditional Management | Salt Management |
|---|---|---|
| Group Custom States | Unsupported | Supported |
| Organization Custom States | Unsupported | Supported |
| System Set Manager | Supported | Supported |
| Service Pack Migration | Supported | Supported |
| Virtualization Host Management: *Auto-installation/bare metal installation support* | Supported | Coming Soon |
| System Redeployment: *With Auto-installation* | Supported | Coming Soon |
| Contact Methods: *How the server communicates with a client* | osad, rhnsd, ssh push, Supported | zeromq: Salt default<br>salt-ssh: Coming Soon |
| Red Hat Network Clients *RHEL 6, 7* | Supported | Supported |
| SUSE Manager Proxy | Supported | Supported |
| Action Chains | Supported | Unsupported |
| Software Crash Reporting | Supported | Unsupported |
| Staging | Supported | Under Review |
| Duplicate Package Reporting *Example: Multiple Versions of the Linux Kernel* | Supported | Coming Soon |
| SCAP Auditing | Supported | Coming Soon |
| Support for Multiple Organizations | Supported with Isolation Enforcement ** | Supported without Isolation Enforcement ** |

| Feature/Function | Traditional Management | Salt Management |
|---|---|---|
| Package Verification | Supported | Under Review |
| System Locking | Supported | Under Review |
| Configuration File Management | Supported | Supported (Tech Preview) |
| Snapshots and Profiles | Supported | Under Review |
| Power Management | Supported | Coming Soon |

 ## Warning: Isolation Enforcement **

In SUSE Manager 2.1 organizations are multi-tenant and completely isolated from one another. This isolation includes both privacy and security. For example: User A in Org_1 cannot see user B in Org_2. (This relates to any data specific to an organization including: servers, channels, activation keys, configuration channels, files and so on.)

In SUSE Manager 3.1 Salt currently does not support any level of multi-tenancy and therefore information specific to an organization is accessible across organizations. For example:

```
salt '*' cmd.run "some_dangerous_command"
```

The above command will target all organization, groups and single systems including their files, channels, activation keys etc. This should be kept in mind when working with Salt.

The following table provides an overview of differences in functionality between SUSE Manager 2.1 and 3.1.

TABLE 19.2: COMPARING SUSE MANAGER 2.1 AND 3.1 FUNCTIONALITY

| Functionality | SUSE Manager 2.1 | SUSE Manager 3.1 |
|---|---|---|
| Configuration Management | Based on Static Configuration | Redesigned with Salt Integration |
| Configuration Management | No Concept of States | States are Supported |

| Functionality | SUSE Manager 2.1 | SUSE Manager 3.1 |
| --- | --- | --- |
| Subscription Management | Limited Functionality | New Design, Full Featured |
| Monitoring | Traditional Monitoring Supported until End of Life | Nagios Compatible, Icinga Monitoring Server is Included |
| Installation Approach | Appliance Based | Installed as an Add-on |
| Compatibility | Compatibility Carried Forward to SUSE Manager 3 | Maintains full SUSE Manager 2.1 Functionality *Traditional Monitoring Removed* |

# A GNU Licenses

This appendix contains the GNU Free Documentation License version 1.2.

## GNU Free Documentation License

Copyright (C) 2000, 2001, 2002 Free Software Foundation, Inc. 51 Franklin St, Fifth Floor, Boston, MA 02110-1301 USA. Everyone is permitted to copy and distribute verbatim copies of this license document, but changing it is not allowed.

## 0. PREAMBLE

The purpose of this License is to make a manual, textbook, or other functional and useful document "free" in the sense of freedom: to assure everyone the effective freedom to copy and redistribute it, with or without modifying it, either commercially or noncommercially. Secondarily, this License preserves for the author and publisher a way to get credit for their work, while not being considered responsible for modifications made by others.

This License is a kind of "copyleft", which means that derivative works of the document must themselves be free in the same sense. It complements the GNU General Public License, which is a copyleft license designed for free software.

We have designed this License in order to use it for manuals for free software, because free software needs free documentation: a free program should come with manuals providing the same freedoms that the software does. But this License is not limited to software manuals; it can be used for any textual work, regardless of subject matter or whether it is published as a printed book. We recommend this License principally for works whose purpose is instruction or reference.

## 1. APPLICABILITY AND DEFINITIONS

This License applies to any manual or other work, in any medium, that contains a notice placed by the copyright holder saying it can be distributed under the terms of this License. Such a notice grants a world-wide, royalty-free license, unlimited in duration, to use that work under the conditions stated herein. The "Document", below, refers to any such manual or work. Any member of the public is a licensee, and is addressed as "you". You accept the license if you copy, modify or distribute the work in a way requiring permission under copyright law.

A "Modified Version" of the Document means any work containing the Document or a portion of it, either copied verbatim, or with modifications and/or translated into another language.

A "Secondary Section" is a named appendix or a front-matter section of the Document that deals exclusively with the relationship of the publishers or authors of the Document to the Document's overall subject (or to related matters) and contains nothing that could fall directly within that overall subject. (Thus, if the Document is in part a textbook of mathematics, a Secondary Section may not explain any mathematics.) The relationship could be a matter of historical connection with the subject or with related matters, or of legal, commercial, philosophical, ethical or political position regarding them.

The "Invariant Sections" are certain Secondary Sections whose titles are designated, as being those of Invariant Sections, in the notice that says that the Document is released under this License. If a section does not fit the above definition of Secondary then it is not allowed to be designated as Invariant. The Document may contain zero Invariant Sections. If the Document does not identify any Invariant Sections then there are none.

The "Cover Texts" are certain short passages of text that are listed, as Front-Cover Texts or Back-Cover Texts, in the notice that says that the Document is released under this License. A Front-Cover Text may be at most 5 words, and a Back-Cover Text may be at most 25 words.

A "Transparent" copy of the Document means a machine-readable copy, represented in a format whose specification is available to the general public, that is suitable for revising the document straightforwardly with generic text editors or (for images composed of pixels) generic paint programs or (for drawings) some widely available drawing editor, and that is suitable for input to text formatters or for automatic translation to a variety of formats suitable for input to text formatters. A copy made in an otherwise Transparent file format whose markup, or absence of markup, has been arranged to thwart or discourage subsequent modification by readers is not Transparent. An image format is not Transparent if used for any substantial amount of text. A copy that is not "Transparent" is called "Opaque".

Examples of suitable formats for Transparent copies include plain ASCII without markup, Texinfo input format, LaTeX input format, SGML or XML using a publicly available DTD, and standard-conforming simple HTML, PostScript or PDF designed for human modification. Examples of transparent image formats include PNG, XCF and JPG. Opaque formats include proprietary formats that can be read and edited only by proprietary word processors, SGML or XML for which the DTD and/or processing tools are not generally available, and the machine-generated HTML, PostScript or PDF produced by some word processors for output purposes only.

The "Title Page" means, for a printed book, the title page itself, plus such following pages as are needed to hold, legibly, the material this License requires to appear in the title page. For works in formats which do not have any title page as such, "Title Page" means the text near the most prominent appearance of the work's title, preceding the beginning of the body of the text.

A section "Entitled XYZ" means a named subunit of the Document whose title either is precisely XYZ or contains XYZ in parentheses following text that translates XYZ in another language. (Here XYZ stands for a specific section name mentioned below, such as "Acknowledgements", "Dedications", "Endorsements", or "History".) To "Preserve the Title" of such a section when you modify the Document means that it remains a section "Entitled XYZ" according to this definition.

The Document may include Warranty Disclaimers next to the notice which states that this License applies to the Document. These Warranty Disclaimers are considered to be included by reference in this License, but only as regards disclaiming warranties: any other implication that these Warranty Disclaimers may have is void and has no effect on the meaning of this License.

## 2. VERBATIM COPYING

You may copy and distribute the Document in any medium, either commercially or noncommercially, provided that this License, the copyright notices, and the license notice saying this License applies to the Document are reproduced in all copies, and that you add no other conditions whatsoever to those of this License. You may not use technical measures to obstruct or control the reading or further copying of the copies you make or distribute. However, you may accept compensation in exchange for copies. If you distribute a large enough number of copies you must also follow the conditions in section 3.

You may also lend copies, under the same conditions stated above, and you may publicly display copies.

## 3. COPYING IN QUANTITY

If you publish printed copies (or copies in media that commonly have printed covers) of the Document, numbering more than 100, and the Document's license notice requires Cover Texts, you must enclose the copies in covers that carry, clearly and legibly, all these Cover Texts: Front-Cover Texts on the front cover, and Back-Cover Texts on the back cover. Both covers must also clearly and legibly identify you as the publisher of these copies. The front cover must present the full title with all words of the title equally prominent and visible. You may add other material on the covers in addition. Copying with changes limited to the covers, as long as they preserve the title of the Document and satisfy these conditions, can be treated as verbatim copying in other respects.

If the required texts for either cover are too voluminous to fit legibly, you should put the first ones listed (as many as fit reasonably) on the actual cover, and continue the rest onto adjacent pages.

If you publish or distribute Opaque copies of the Document numbering more than 100, you must either include a machine-readable Transparent copy along with each Opaque copy, or state in or with each Opaque copy a computer-network location from which the general network-using public has access to download using public-standard network protocols a complete Transparent copy of the Document, free of added material. If you use the latter option, you must take reasonably prudent steps, when you begin distribution of Opaque copies in quantity, to ensure that this Transparent copy will remain thus accessible at the stated location until at least one year after the last time you distribute an Opaque copy (directly or through your agents or retailers) of that edition to the public.

It is requested, but not required, that you contact the authors of the Document well before redistributing any large number of copies, to give them a chance to provide you with an updated version of the Document.

## 4. MODIFICATIONS

You may copy and distribute a Modified Version of the Document under the conditions of sections 2 and 3 above, provided that you release the Modified Version under precisely this License, with the Modified Version filling the role of the Document, thus licensing distribution and modification of the Modified Version to whoever possesses a copy of it. In addition, you must do these things in the Modified Version:

A. Use in the Title Page (and on the covers, if any) a title distinct from that of the Document, and from those of previous versions (which should, if there were any, be listed in the History section of the Document). You may use the same title as a previous version if the original publisher of that version gives permission.

B. List on the Title Page, as authors, one or more persons or entities responsible for authorship of the modifications in the Modified Version, together with at least five of the principal authors of the Document (all of its principal authors, if it has fewer than five), unless they release you from this requirement.

C. State on the Title page the name of the publisher of the Modified Version, as the publisher.

D. Preserve all the copyright notices of the Document.

E. Add an appropriate copyright notice for your modifications adjacent to the other copyright notices.

F. Include, immediately after the copyright notices, a license notice giving the public permission to use the Modified Version under the terms of this License, in the form shown in the Addendum below.

G. Preserve in that license notice the full lists of Invariant Sections and required Cover Texts given in the Document's license notice.

H. Include an unaltered copy of this License.

I. Preserve the section Entitled "History", Preserve its Title, and add to it an item stating at least the title, year, new authors, and publisher of the Modified Version as given on the Title Page. If there is no section Entitled "History" in the Document, create one stating the title, year, authors, and publisher of the Document as given on its Title Page, then add an item describing the Modified Version as stated in the previous sentence.

J. Preserve the network location, if any, given in the Document for public access to a Transparent copy of the Document, and likewise the network locations given in the Document for previous versions it was based on. These may be placed in the "History" section. You may omit a network location for a work that was published at least four years before the Document itself, or if the original publisher of the version it refers to gives permission.

K. For any section Entitled "Acknowledgements" or "Dedications", Preserve the Title of the section, and preserve in the section all the substance and tone of each of the contributor acknowledgements and/or dedications given therein.

L. Preserve all the Invariant Sections of the Document, unaltered in their text and in their titles. Section numbers or the equivalent are not considered part of the section titles.

M. Delete any section Entitled "Endorsements". Such a section may not be included in the Modified Version.

N. Do not retitle any existing section to be Entitled "Endorsements" or to conflict in title with any Invariant Section.

O. Preserve any Warranty Disclaimers.

If the Modified Version includes new front-matter sections or appendices that qualify as Secondary Sections and contain no material copied from the Document, you may at your option designate some or all of these sections as invariant. To do this, add their titles to the list of Invariant Sections in the Modified Version's license notice. These titles must be distinct from any other section titles.

You may add a section Entitled "Endorsements", provided it contains nothing but endorsements of your Modified Version by various parties--for example, statements of peer review or that the text has been approved by an organization as the authoritative definition of a standard.

You may add a passage of up to five words as a Front-Cover Text, and a passage of up to 25 words as a Back-Cover Text, to the end of the list of Cover Texts in the Modified Version. Only one passage of Front-Cover Text and one of Back-Cover Text may be added by (or through arrangements made by) any one entity. If the Document already includes a cover text for the same cover, previously added by you or by arrangement made by the same entity you are acting on behalf of, you may not add another; but you may replace the old one, on explicit permission from the previous publisher that added the old one.

The author(s) and publisher(s) of the Document do not by this License give permission to use their names for publicity for or to assert or imply endorsement of any Modified Version.

## 5. COMBINING DOCUMENTS

You may combine the Document with other documents released under this License, under the terms defined in section 4 above for modified versions, provided that you include in the combination all of the Invariant Sections of all of the original documents, unmodified, and list them all as Invariant Sections of your combined work in its license notice, and that you preserve all their Warranty Disclaimers.

The combined work need only contain one copy of this License, and multiple identical Invariant Sections may be replaced with a single copy. If there are multiple Invariant Sections with the same name but different contents, make the title of each such section unique by adding at the end of it, in parentheses, the name of the original author or publisher of that section if known, or else a unique number. Make the same adjustment to the section titles in the list of Invariant Sections in the license notice of the combined work.

In the combination, you must combine any sections Entitled "History" in the various original documents, forming one section Entitled "History"; likewise combine any sections Entitled "Acknowledgements", and any sections Entitled "Dedications". You must delete all sections Entitled "Endorsements".

## 6. COLLECTIONS OF DOCUMENTS

You may make a collection consisting of the Document and other documents released under this License, and replace the individual copies of this License in the various documents with a single copy that is included in the collection, provided that you follow the rules of this License for verbatim copying of each of the documents in all other respects.

You may extract a single document from such a collection, and distribute it individually under this License, provided you insert a copy of this License into the extracted document, and follow this License in all other respects regarding verbatim copying of that document.

## 7. AGGREGATION WITH INDEPENDENT WORKS

A compilation of the Document or its derivatives with other separate and independent documents or works, in or on a volume of a storage or distribution medium, is called an "aggregate" if the copyright resulting from the compilation is not used to limit the legal rights of the compilation's users beyond what the individual works permit. When the Document is included in an aggregate, this License does not apply to the other works in the aggregate which are not themselves derivative works of the Document.

If the Cover Text requirement of section 3 is applicable to these copies of the Document, then if the Document is less than one half of the entire aggregate, the Document's Cover Texts may be placed on covers that bracket the Document within the aggregate, or the electronic equivalent of covers if the Document is in electronic form. Otherwise they must appear on printed covers that bracket the whole aggregate.

## 8. TRANSLATION

Translation is considered a kind of modification, so you may distribute translations of the Document under the terms of section 4. Replacing Invariant Sections with translations requires special permission from their copyright holders, but you may include translations of some or all Invariant Sections in addition to the original versions of these Invariant Sections. You may include a translation of this License, and all the license notices in the Document, and any Warranty Disclaimers, provided that you also include the original English version of this License and the original versions of those notices and disclaimers. In case of a disagreement between the translation and the original version of this License or a notice or disclaimer, the original version will prevail.

If a section in the Document is Entitled "Acknowledgements", "Dedications", or "History", the requirement (section 4) to Preserve its Title (section 1) will typically require changing the actual title.

## 9. TERMINATION

You may not copy, modify, sublicense, or distribute the Document except as expressly provided for under this License. Any other attempt to copy, modify, sublicense or distribute the Document is void, and will automatically terminate your rights under this License. However, parties who have received copies, or rights, from you under this License will not have their licenses terminated so long as such parties remain in full compliance.

## 10. FUTURE REVISIONS OF THIS LICENSE

The Free Software Foundation may publish new, revised versions of the GNU Free Documentation License from time to time. Such new versions will be similar in spirit to the present version, but may differ in detail to address new problems or concerns. See http://www.gnu.org/copyleft/ .

Each version of the License is given a distinguishing version number. If the Document specifies that a particular numbered version of this License "or any later version" applies to it, you have the option of following the terms and conditions either of that specified version or of any later version that has been published (not as a draft) by the Free Software Foundation. If the Document does not specify a version number of this License, you may choose any version ever published (not as a draft) by the Free Software Foundation.

## ADDENDUM: How to use this License for your documents

```
Copyright (c) YEAR YOUR NAME.
Permission is granted to copy, distribute and/or modify this document
under the terms of the GNU Free Documentation License, Version 1.2
or any later version published by the Free Software Foundation;
with no Invariant Sections, no Front-Cover Texts, and no Back-Cover Texts.
A copy of the license is included in the section entitled "GNU
Free Documentation License".
```

If you have Invariant Sections, Front-Cover Texts and Back-Cover Texts, replace the "with...Texts." line with this:

```
with the Invariant Sections being LIST THEIR TITLES, with the
Front-Cover Texts being LIST, and with the Back-Cover Texts being LIST.
```

If you have Invariant Sections without Cover Texts, or some other combination of the three, merge those two alternatives to suit the situation.

If your document contains nontrivial examples of program code, we recommend releasing these examples in parallel under your choice of free software license, such as the GNU General Public License, to permit their use in free software.

www.ingramcontent.com/pod-product-compliance
Lightning Source LLC
Chambersburg PA
CBHW082120070326
40690CB00049B/4016